PRAISE FOR WEDDIN
CEREMONY H

"Mark's book not only epitomizes his commitment to his craft, but also demonstrates his desire to help the rest of us overcome our ceremony jitters and serve as officiant with total confidence, reverence, and joy. I met Mark as our two worlds collided–his teaching wedding officiant success, and mine teaching mobile notary and loan signing agent success. It's the perfect marriage of industries and passions! (See what I did there?)

What truly bonded us, though, is our mutual passion for teaching others. On both fronts, the work matters! As a wedding officiant, whether your couple asked you as a friend or hired you as a professional, you're being counted on to help make their nuptials special. Give your couples, their guests, and yourself the gift of learning from the best so you can deliver a ceremony they will remember forever. Read this book! In fact, read the whole series!"

BILL SOROKA, FOUNDER OF NOTARYCOACH.COM & AUTHOR OF SIGN & THRIVE: HOW TO MAKE SIX FIGURES AS A MOBILE NOTARY AND LOAN SIGNING AGENT

"More and more, modern couples are enlisting the help of a dear friend or relative to marry them. To pronounce them married. It's a big job, and you're the chosen one for the job of officiant or celebrant. You need this guide!

In Mark Allan Groleau, you have an expert officiant guiding you step by step as you craft and execute a modern wedding ceremony. Seriously, we call on Mark quite often and we cannot sing his praises enough. If we were getting married, we'd want Mark to marry us!

Whether you are a layman or a professional, this will help you be the best damn wedding officiant you can be. So go ahead - marry your friends! We believe in you, and we believe in Mark's process."

CHRISTY MATTHEWS & MICHELLE MARTINEZ,
HOSTS/PRODUCERS OF THE BIG WEDDING PLANNING
PODCAST & THE BIG WEDDING PLANNING MASTER CLASS

WEDDING ZERO TO CEREMONY HERO

LEARN THE BASICS, PLAN THE CEREMONY, AND WRITE THE WEDDING THEY'VE ALWAYS WANTED

MARK ALLAN GROLEAU

Copyright © 2021 by Mark Allan Groleau

All rights reserved.

No part of this book may be reproduced in any form or by any electronic or mechanical means, including information storage and retrieval systems, without written permission from the author, except for the use of brief quotations in a book review.

For Naomi, Oka, and Zane. You're my Why.

CONTENTS

| Free Resource | 11 |
| Introduction | 13 |

PART ONE: LEARN THE BASICS

THE CLASSIC 10-PART WEDDING CEREMONY	23
1. Officiant Entrance	23
2. The Processional	24
3. Officiant's Speech and Question of Intent	25
4. Vows	25
5. Ring Exchange	26
6. Pronouncement of the Couple	26
7. Signing of the Registry	27
8. Closing Remarks	27
9. Presentation of the Couple	27
10. Recessional	28

PART TWO: PLAN THE CEREMONY

| ONE: START THE WORKSHOP | 33 |
| Two Things to Tell Your Couple | 33 |

TWO: COVER THE LOGISTICAL DETAILS	36
Couple's Names?	36
Ceremony Date and Time?	38
Rehearsal Date and Time?	38
Cast of Characters?	39
Microphones	40
1. How Many Guests?	40
2. Indoor or Outdoor?	41
3. What Style of Mic for Officiant?	41
4. Does the Couple Need a Mic for Vows?	42
5. Any Readers who Need Mics?	43

THREE: PLAN THE PRE-CEREMONY	44
Fifteen Minutes before Ceremony Start	44
Will Partner A and Partner B Be Doing a "First Look"?	44

Where Are Partner A and Their Party?	45
Where Are Partner B and Their Party?	45
Who Is Playing Pre-ceremony Music?	46
Who Is Greeting Guests at the Door?	46
FOUR: BRAINSTORM THE ELEMENTS OF THE CEREMONY	47
Ceremony Kickoff	47
Is Anyone Escorting Partner B Down the Aisle in the Processional?	49
Is Partner A's Party Walking in the Processional, or Only Partner B's?	49
Is There Special Honorary Seating for the Parents or Grandparents?	50
How Does the Officiant Enter?	50
How and When Does Partner A Enter?	51
Order of Partner A's Entry?	51
Opening Remarks	53
What Is the Couple's Preference about Photo-Taking?	53
Is There Anything Else the Guests Need to Know besides "Silence Your Devices"?	53
Ceremony Music	54
Processional Song?	54
Separate Song for Partner B?	54
Signing Song?	55
Recessional Song?	55
Any Other Music?	56
Processional	56
Full Order of All Friends and Family Processing?	56
Kids in the Processional	57
How Far to the Front until Partner A Steps Forward to Receive Partner B?	59
Is the Handoff to Music or The Question?	60
Is There a Bouquet Handoff? To Whom?	62
Will Someone Need to Arrange Partner B's Dress?	62
Elements	63
Has a Significant Family Member Passed Away Who We Would Like to Acknowledge?	63
Are There Any Readings or Prayers by Friends or Family? Who and When?	64
Any Religious Elements Like Prayers or Blessings by the Officiant or Someone Else?	65

Are There Any Other Rituals in the Ceremony? By Whom and When?	66
The "Big Three" Rituals	68
Unity Candle	69
Sand Mixing	69
Handfasting	70
Are There Any Custom Elements?	72
Vows Style: Write/Read Own, Repeat, or Simple "I Do"?	73
Style #1: Write and Read Your Own Vows	73
Style #2: Repeat Line-by-Line	75
Style #3: Just Say "I Do"	76
(Bonus!) Style #4: Hybrid	76
Who Is Holding the Rings?	77
Pronouncement: "Husband/Wife" or "Married"?	77
Pronouncement: You May Kiss Your Bride/Groom? Or Something Else?	78
Registry Signing	78
Who Are the Signing Witnesses?	82
Will We Be at a Table with Chairs or a High-Top?	82
If Sitting, Do Both Partner A and Partner B Sit? Or Just Partner A?	82
Option 1: Two Chairs; Only the Couple Sit.	83
Option 2: Two Chairs; First the Couple Sit, Then the Witnesses.	83
Option 3: One Chair; Only the Bride Sits.	83
Option 4: One Chair; Only the Wedding Couple Take Turns Sitting	83
Option 5: One Chair; Only the Bride and the Maid of Honour Sit.	84
Not Recommended: Everyone Takes a Turn	84
Officiant Gives the Couple's Portion of the Licence to Whom?	85
Closing Remarks	86
What Are the Newlyweds Doing Next?	86
What Do the Guests Need to Do Now?	86
Wording for the Presentation of the Couple?	87
Recessional	88
FIVE: TELL YOUR COUPLE WHAT'S COMING NEXT	89

PART THREE: WRITE THE SCRIPT

START THE ONLY SCRIPT YOU'LL EVER WRITE	93
MAKE THE SCRIPT LOOK LIKE A PLAY	94

MAKE THE SCRIPT EASY TO READ	97
CLEARLY MARK THE OUTSTANDING ITEMS	100
USE COLLABORATIVE SOFTWARE AND SEND THE SCRIPT	101
Next	104
Appendix	107
Acknowledgments	111
About the Author	113
Online Course	115

FREE RESOURCE

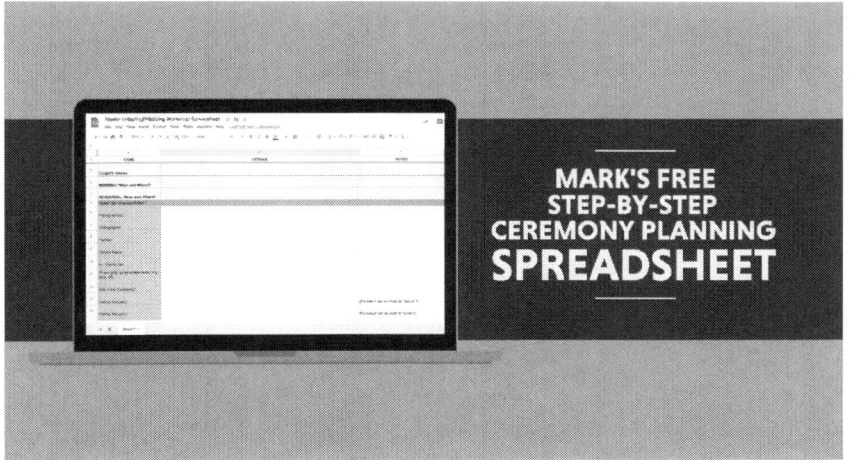

Free Ceremony Planning Spreadsheet: get your very own copy of the step-by-step planning spreadsheet, covered in this book. Claim it as a free gift and follow along here:
www.unboringweddingacademy.com/spreadsheet

INTRODUCTION

So you wanna officiate[1] this wedding. Maybe only because you couldn't get out of it! Whether you're overjoyed or you're over a barrel, you said yes anyways. Your first thought was, "What an honour to officiate a wedding!" Your very next thought was, "Wait—what? How?" And here you are.

You're sitting at Square Zero. The starting block. There are a couple of things people do in your position. Some make it up based on all the weddings they've seen. They wing it. They write some sort of ceremony, charge out there, and see if it works. Others copy a script from the internet and assume that'll do just fine. They paste it, charge out there, and see if it works. We have our wing-it officiants and our paste-it officiants. Both options result in an "okay" wedding ceremony at best.

You don't fit into either one of those categories. You're reading this book. You're taking the time and effort to consult, because you want to get this 100% right.

You remind me of the winners of a contest I got to help out with a few years ago. I watched as the teams waited to start. Everyone was visibly nervous, wringing their hands and taking deep breaths. Their task was difficult. Before time ran out, they had to race across the hot desert to the gold mine, dig out as much gold as they could, and get back with more gold than the other teams. All without running out of food or water. The team who made it back with the most gold would be the winner.

The contest marshal rang the starting bell and Turn One began. They were off. Several turns in, a quarter of the teams ran out of food and starved. Soon, another quarter ran out of water and died of thirst. Others had all their equipment wiped out in sandstorms. Some made it to the gold mine, stayed for a day or two, and rushed back to safety with only a handful of treasure. A few made it to the mine, stayed too long and gathered too much, and couldn't get back in time. When the marshal announced the final turn, one team was the clear winner. They were the only team that got the right supplies, survived the dust storms, made it to the mine, got the perfect amount of gold, and returned before their food and water ran out.

How did they do it? When the marshal took the stage again, she playfully scolded the teams who lost. (Yes. This was an experiential learning game for employees of a major corporation. We weren't in the desert.) She'd seen this play out in every one of the games she'd hosted week in and week out, and this one was no different. One factor that always separated the winners from the losers. One decision that took them from Turn Zero to gold-mining heroes.

"Do you remember what I told you before the game started?" she asked.

She'd announced that they could use their first few turns drawing cards from one of the game facilitators. Each card would have a piece of wisdom from the local wise man written on it. The local wise man knew the desert. He knew the mines. He knew the weather patterns. The intel on those cards would inform the reader how much gold it would take to win. It would tell them how many turns they should spend at the mine. How often sandstorms struck. How to make the most of their supplies.

Many of the teams hadn't even heard the marshal say any of this. They'd started talking and discussing their own strategy with each other while she was still giving instructions! The vast majority of the teams were off like shots on Turn One and were at the mines or halfway there by Turn Five. The winning team had listened carefully to all her instructions. Well into the game, they were still parked at Square Zero, burning their turns and collecting knowledge from the local wise man.

I happened to be the facilitator for the winning table. I was the one handing them their cards. It took nerves of steel for them to sit there turn after turn asking for one card at a time while the other teams were mining their gold and whooping it up all around them. It took resolve and a stomach for risk. *All the others are already there. Am I making a huge mistake?* Their decision to listen and wait turned out to be the game-changer for the challenges that awaited them between Turn Zero and coming home a hero. Between winning the game or dying in the desert. The team that won was the team that spent the most turns consulting the local wise man.

That's you. Reading this book will skyrocket your likelihood of doing a *great* job—not just an okay job. You're burning turns figuring out how to do this well for you and your couple. That takes guts. After all, it makes sense to assume that consulting the local wise man takes up too much time and resources. But guess what. There are hundreds of details between now and the wedding. Things you have no clue about yet. Your good decision here is not only going to save you time and prevent costly errors; it means you're going to wildly succeed.

On your officiating journey, I'm the grizzled old local wise man who's going to tell you, step by step, what you need to know. Maybe you set out on this wedding ceremony adventure hoping to come back with just a handful of gold. Or maybe you would have been happy to just get out of this alive! Don't settle for that, friend. Shoot for Hero! Finish this book, and you're going to write the customized ceremony your couple wants. You're blasting off—from Wedding Zero to Ceremony Hero.

Using This Book: Ceremony Hero

When my friends asked me to officiate their wedding, it was my first. I'd never done it before. I was scared. It wasn't standing up in front of people and talking that scared me; I'd done a lot of that. What scared me was the wedding protocol. It was the spectre of letting my couple down. It was the seriousness of the whole thing. It was the idea that there was a right way to do it and a wrong way. That if I deviated, everyone would think that I was an impostor or a hack—or worse: the couple wouldn't even be legally married!

As it turns out, I survived that first ceremony. But I'd felt too sick with worry and uncertainty to enjoy it the way I could have. I didn't know anything about wedding protocol. I didn't even know how to talk to my first couple about what they wanted in their ceremony.

I don't want that for you. First, I'll let you in on a not-so-little secret. The idea of wedding protocol is mostly a myth nowadays. Sure, there are certain traditions. And we use that as a loose framework. We still want the wedding to be recognizable as a *wedding*, after all. But in my first dozen wedding rehearsals, I was shocked to see wedding planners change almost anything and everything their couple didn't want or like. Did the bride want to stand on a different side? Fine! Parents wanted to sit on a different side? You bet! Dad and bride want to swap sides in the aisle? Not a problem! "Wait, you can just do that?" I thought. All my paranoia about "the right way" was unnecessary and misguided.

I started taking more charge and following those wedding planners' leads. I found the courage to ask my couples what they wanted and what they didn't want in their ceremony. Soon, all my fears about officiating melted away. Then I started honing a process. In just one sharp, well-run meeting with your couple, you will expertly extract their vision for their perfect ceremony. Like gold. That's what this book will teach you how to do.

In this book, Part One deals with ceremony basics. But we're not going to let ourselves be constrained by "the way things have always been" in weddings. That's why, in Part Two of this book, you're going to learn how to sit down with your couple and guide them through a tight, well-run, one-hour ceremony planning meeting. Coming out of that meeting, you'll have all the information you need to build the ceremony. Then in Part Three, you'll learn how to write and format the professional, custom-made wedding script your couple has always wanted. At the end of this book you'll be able to navigate the details of a wedding ceremony, rock a planning session with your couple, and deliver the script your couple wants.

This book is *not* a wham-bam filing cabinet of canned scripts for you to copy and paste. There are other places you can find that. It's not a data dump of wedding instructions, either. *Wedding Zero to Ceremony Hero* is a step-by-step process. My goal in this book is to teach you two things at once. First: as you read, you'll be learning all the ins and outs of a wedding ceremony–down to the granular details. Second: at the very same time, you'll be transforming yourself into a guide for your couple. This is not something we could achieve by copying and pasting sample scripts. In the pages of this book, *I'm* a ceremony guide for *you*. When you're done this book, *you* will be a ceremony guide for *others*.

Book Two: Unboring!Wedding

But what about the dead seriousness of a wedding ceremony? The mind-numbing boringness of a wedding ceremony? I want to teach you exactly how to obliterate that, too. A wedding that your couple and their guests will *rave* about takes more than just getting the elements right. There's a technique to unleashing everyone's laughter and happy tears. You *can and will* knock their socks off with tasteful playfulness and a masterfully written love story.

The full Unboring!Wedding method is a three-book series. It's a chronological pathway for you to follow. In the next book, we're going to build on the foundation we laid in this one. Book Two spills all my secrets in a single Unboring!Wedding Formula. It'll punch up your wedding script to make you one of the best officiants anyone's ever seen. Do I mean "not-bad-for-an-amateur" best? Nope. I mean no-one-can-tell-it's-your-first-time best. I mean you'll be one of the greats—on your first try.

How can I make such a bold claim? Because I've taught this exact system to hundreds of first-time officiants and celebrants all over the world with my online course *Unboring!Wedding Academy*. My first-time-officiant clients have all come back with staggering reviews from their couples and wedding guests. "Everyone. Was. Raving!"

With my Unboring!Wedding Formula in your hands, you'll be one of those elites. One of the few wise enough to take the time to prepare and learn a proven, A–Z method from a seasoned professional. And just like *this* book, in the next one you'll simply follow the step-by-step system my clients and I use to melt faces at our weddings week in and week out.

Book Three: Unboring!Wedding Pro

During the spring of the global pandemic, I taught a live video version of my online course *Unboring!Wedding Academy*. We took a span of six weeks. As the course progressed, a number of the students started asking me things like, "Mark, how do I find clients?" and "How do you respond to cold enquiries from couples?" and "How do we network with wedding pros?"

I told them my course didn't include that. Like this book, *Unboring!Wedding Academy* only covers my method to craft and deliver the best wedding ceremony anyone's ever seen. Jeez, no big deal, right? I told them not everyone cares about that other business-y stuff. I want everything in the course to be for everyone, not just would-be pros. A lot of people just want to deliver a great ceremony for their daughter or nephew or best friend. That's who this book and that course are for. But the course cohort started ganging up on me in the chat. "Well, Mark, you sure as heck better create a second course for us right away, then!" And with that, *Unboring!Wedding Academy: Pro* was born.

That's what we'll cover in Book Three: going pro as a wedding officiant. After Book Two, you'll be able to write and deliver a face-melting wedding ceremony. But how do you do it over and over again? For couples you've never met? With the top wedding vendors in your market? How do you find clients? How do you get referrals and online traffic and deposits and a written contract? How do you automate that flow and manage all those weddings? If you're thinking of going pro, you'll follow my step-by-step process in Book Three. It's the exact process I used in growing to a full-time officiating practice. It's what I do to keep booking couples and scoring perfect reviews year after year.

Enough about the future. Let's talk about the present. Are you ready to deliver a fun, thrilling ceremony experience for your couple and all their guests? To go from Wedding Zero to Ceremony Hero? Then the step-by-step system in this book is the road for you. And we start with the basics.

---

1. "Officiant" and "officiate" are the terms most frequently used in North America, and "celebrant" is the term used in other places. For the purposes of this book, I'm unfortunately forced to use one or the other. To use both would be exhausting or confusing for the reader. For consistency, and with apologies to those for whom "celebrant" is more appropriate, I've chosen my own more local North American terms "officiant" and "officiate." Only out of necessity, I promise.

PART ONE: LEARN THE BASICS

When I say the word "Picasso," I'll bet an image comes to mind: a contorted painting of a face made up of wild shapes all mashed together. Whatever you think of Picasso's work, he is widely regarded as one of the world's greatest artists, along with Monet and Van Gogh and others. But Picasso didn't pick up a brush one day and say, "I'm gonna make a picture out of shapes!" Picasso started in art school. He studied the old Renaissance masters and their "linear perspective." He educated himself in the methods that had set the tone for all the art of the last four hundred years before him. He learned to paint as the legacy masters had painted. Then he began to deviate a little from the old ways. And then a lot. Before long, Picasso brought the ideas and the spirit of his time to the canvas. He spawned a whole new style of painting and art called cubism. He changed fine art forever, and now he's a household name.

"Learn the rules like a pro so you can break them like an artist." A lot of people attribute this quote to Picasso. Even though he probably didn't ever say it, it's attributed to Picasso because Picasso knew the rules and broke them well. First, he learned the elementary methods of traditional painting. Then he twisted the whole medium enough to make it his own and change it forever.

Remember when you started learning something you had no clue about? (Okay, before officiating a wedding.) When you learn a thing from zero, first you learn the technicalities of it. You start with books and learning proper forms and copying the methods already out there. You have no feel for a golf swing or a yoga flow or how to change a diaper when it's new to you. So, you follow the exact steps the teacher tells you and shows you. And after you do it enough times, an intuitive feel starts to develop. Before long, you're bending the rules a bit. You're adding your own style. (I'm not sure diaper changing is an art form, but my kids, well…)

I want you to deliver a wedding ceremony with such flair and style that it becomes "yours." We are making art, after all. To get there, though, we have to go from Step Zero to Step One. Before we learn the tips and hacks for the best ceremony anyone's ever seen, we need to start with the basics. We need to start with the conventional Western wedding ceremony as we know and (may not) love it: the Classic 10-part Wedding Ceremony. After this, we'll discuss in Part Two of this book exactly how to run a single 60-minute planning session with your couple. In that meeting, you'll extract everything you need from your couple to write the exact ceremony they've always wanted. But that's later. Let's start at the Renaissance, and then go full Picasso.

THE CLASSIC 10-PART WEDDING CEREMONY

1. Officiant Entrance

You can't teleport into a wedding ceremony (yet), so you gotta walk to the front somehow. The scene in the minutes before a ceremony typically looks like this: the guests are chatting across the aisle. Some folks are in their seats, but others are still standing around. The DJ or live band is playing light prelude music to set the vibe. No one is paying attention. There's no trumpet blast that signals that we're about to start. There's no announcement, either: "Ladies and Gentlemen, boys and girls…!" Nope. What signals that the ceremony is about to start is the officiant's entrance. See how important you are?

You will typically come to the front in one of three ways. In the first option, the officiant walks in alone. In the second option, the officiant walks in with Wedding Partner A[1] (the bride or groom who is *not* walking down the aisle in the processional). In the third option, the officiant walks in with Wedding Partner A and his or her wedding party.

In Part Two of this book, we drill down deeper into walking our couple through all their ceremony preferences. We'll help them make the best choices for them. All you need to know right now is you're going to kick things off by marching to the front of the room.

2. The Processional

Traditionally, the officiant gets to the front and then the processional music begins. This is the cue for the family and wedding party at the back to make their entrances. The processional is the second major part of a classic wedding ceremony. When the processional music begins, any parents in the processional enter and take their seats. They're followed by junior wedding party members entering one at a time. Then the members of Partner B's party enter and take their places at the front. Finally, the ring bearers come in, and they're followed by the flower girls, and the flower girls herald Partner B's upcoming entrance. When Partner B is set to make their entrance, the officiant will often say to the guests, "Please stand for [Bride or Groom] as you're able." Everyone stands. Traditionally, a parent or family member escorts Partner B on their arm. Sometimes the couple will decide that the processional music will change here for Partner B's entrance and their walk down the aisle.

When Partner B arrives at the front, it has been the custom (in days of yore) for the officiant to ask, "Who gives this woman to be married to this man today?" Some brides want to keep this wording for the sake of tradition (or for their father's wishes). In the 21st century we have same-sex weddings and a lot of women who don't love the idea of being "given away" as property. There are a couple of updated options here.

An alternative second option is to ask a more contemporary version of the question like, "Bruce, do you support Angela's marriage to Cameron today?" Here we're asking for support and blessing, not giving away. A third option is to scrap the question altogether. We will go over these in more detail in the Wedding Workshop section. Whether our couple opts for a question or no question, when that's done, Partner A steps forward to receive Partner B. They take each other by the hand. Then they walk the few remaining paces to the front and centre themselves in front of the officiant.

3. Officiant's Speech and Question of Intent

When the processional is done and the couple are standing at the front, the officiant invites everyone to sit and begins their address. Traditionally this has included an admonition to the couple about the meaning of love and marriage, individual and matrimonial responsibilities, questions to the couple about whether they know of any legal impediment prohibiting their marriage, and whether they stand here today of a sound mind with the intent to marry one another. (And no. People don't listen. Which is why you started skimming that sentence.) However, it's likely you're not a priest who doesn't know these people. In fact, I bet your couple asked you to marry them and you even worked with them to plan and rehearse their ceremony! Imagine that!

I keep only one of the historical relics listed above. It's the question, "Do you stand here today to give yourself to each other in marriage?" I ask this after I tell their love story, and their "we do" answer segues nicely into the next elements of the ceremony. I never lecture about marriage and what they need to do as spouses. It's better to focus on them and on how the promises they're making today are a landmark in their ongoing love story.

That said, you may live in a jurisdiction that requires the officiant to include some specific and brief legal language. You may need to recite specific wording or get them to repeat phrases in order for their wedding to be legally binding. Make sure you find out from your local government what you need to say and do before you jettison the traditional stuff altogether.

4. Vows

The crux of the wedding ceremony is the wedding vows. I'd argue it's not a wedding if the couple don't promise their lives and their faithfulness to each other. Most jurisdictions won't recognize this event as a wedding without the couple exchanging some words of commitment.

There are essentially three ways the couple might choose to say their vows to each other. In Part Two of this book, we'll cover how to coach your couple so they can choose the style of vows that's right for them. The first style is to write and read their own vows to each other. The second style is to repeat after the officiant line by line. For example, the officiant says, "I Cameron, take you Angela," and then Cameron repeats, "I, Cameron, take you, Angela…" The final style is for the officiant to read a question or series of questions to each wedding partner, and they each reply, "I do." Some couples opt for a hybrid of two of these styles. More on that later.

5. Ring Exchange

With the vows exchanged, the officiant leads the couple into exchanging rings. The rings are the physical symbol of the promises. They're a daily reminder of the vows. The officiant will call on the keeper of the rings (the best man) to come forward. That person will then give the ring to Partner A. Partner A will exchange the ring first. After Partner A has the ring, Partner A will put the ring on Partner B's finger, and will repeat some words while giving the ring. Traditionally this part goes, "With this ring, I thee wed." Most couples nowadays prefer less Shakespeare and more present-day vernacular. The ring keeper will then give Partner A's ring to Partner B, and Partner B will do exactly what Partner A did: place it on their finger, and repeat a few words after the officiant.

6. Pronouncement of the Couple

The couple have made their promises and put the rings on each other's fingers. All that's left is for the officiant to pronounce them married. And so, the officiant declares that "by the authority given me," or "by the power vested in me" by such-and-such state and/or church, "…I pronounce you married!" And then comes the big kiss moment. Often the officiant will add, "You may kiss!" And kiss they shall—to the cheers of all the wedding guests.

7. Signing of the Registry

To register this marriage with the government, some papers need to be signed. The officiant, the couple, and typically two witnesses need to fill out an official marriage licence issued by the state or province. Depending on where you're from, you may be saying, "Wait. I've never seen this during the ceremony," or "Wait, I've only ever seen this before the pronouncement of the couple." Yes, I'm aware that in the U.S. it's uncommon to do this in the ceremony. It's more common to do it privately after the ceremony. If you're in a British Commonwealth country, it's common to include it in the ceremony, but to do it before the pronouncement, not after. Later in this book, I'll tell you why I think you should (a) put the signing in the ceremony (looking at you, American friends), and (b) do it after the pronouncement, not before (looking at you, Commonwealth friends). It has to do with making it unboring. For now, let's just say that the signing is an element of the Classic 10-Part Wedding Ceremony that you need to know about. It's up to your couple whether they keep it in, and it's up to you when it happens.

8. Closing Remarks

After the officiant signs the paperwork with the couple and their witnesses, they all go back to front and centre. Then the officiant makes a few remarks about what's happening next. Are the couple heading out for photos or is there a receiving line? Are the guests invited to another space for drinks or dinner, now or later? The officiant tells everyone what's coming next, thanks everyone for coming, and invites everyone to stand for the big finish.

9. Presentation of the Couple

With everyone on their feet, the officiant is ready to wrap up the ceremony with the final grand declaration, "It is my honour to present to you for the very first time…!" The officiant ends that sentence with the appropriate wording: "Mr. and Mrs.…," or "Mr. and Mr.…," or

"Mrs. and Mrs...," or using the new last name, or using first names only, or "husband and wife," or "wife and wife..." You get the picture. There are lots of conjugations and permutations and other "ations" here. However we do it, we present our couple to the world for the first time. As you can probably guess by now, in Part Two we'll cover how to ask our couple what they prefer.

10. Recessional

With that final line, the DJ or the band will strike up the music. The newly-married couple will head up the aisle to a chorus of cheers and applause. When they get all the way up the aisle, the officiant will signal to the wedding parties to recess up the aisle, typically two by two. Then the officiant steps over to the couple's families in the front rows, congratulates them, and invites them to follow the others up the aisle. Then the second row follows, then the third, and so on. And with that, the wedding ceremony is done!

"But wait!" you might be thinking. "You missed the prayer! Or the handfasting! Or the reading! Or the sand mixing! Or the broom jumping! Or the quaich! What about all the other things I've ever seen in a wedding ceremony that you didn't include?"

I'm so glad you asked! There are dozens (if not hundreds!) of elements that a couple can add to a wedding ceremony, depending on their country or tradition or religion or preferences. We'll talk more about that in Part Two of this book. (Are you getting the sense that Part Two is the meat and potatoes?) We're still in the Renaissance stage of wedding ceremonies here, remember? Patience, Picasso! In this chapter we've covered where we start: the Classic 10-Part Ceremony. Now that we've taken the time to learn the necessary basics, we can start playing around with them.

---

1. I aim to use inclusive language in all my communication. For that reason, I refer to the wedding couple as "Partner A and Partner B." An LGBTQ+ couple will choose who starts at the front and who comes down the aisle; it may be one or both or neither. A female/male couple traditionally chooses the groom to begin at the front and the bride to walk down the aisle.

PART TWO: PLAN THE CEREMONY

I've sat across from a lot of brides-to-be. They all want their weddings to be unboring. That's why they call me in the first place. But when we sit down, I notice that brides and grooms all want something else, too.

Nina and her fiancé were just like the others. When I asked her what she wanted for her ceremony (besides unboring), she was quick to answer. "We just don't want any unpleasant surprises like my sister had," Nina told me, her eyes almost pleading. Nina went on to describe how devastated and embarrassed her sister had been at her wedding.

That past summer, Nina had been her sister's maid of honour. As the ceremony started, the officiant read a passage from the Bible. This was a bit strange, but not unusual. Strange because her sister was not at all religious. Not unusual, though, because people read the Bible at weddings. Fine. But then the officiant started to preach. He preached about salvation. And hell. And heaven. Religious ideas that held no interest for Nina's sister and brother-in-law to be. The officiant went on for about fifteen minutes. The bride and groom had assumed the entire ceremony from start to finish would be no more than ten. Meanwhile, the sermon alone was fifteen. Then came the prayer. And then the vows included Nina's sister promising to submit to her husband. Of course, the groom's vows did not call for him to submit. In short, they considered the ceremony a disaster, an embarrassment, and totally out of line with their values. The couple had no idea it would look and sound like that.

"That's why we don't want any surprises," Nina repeated.

I was happy to tell her: I'm all about preventing unpleasant surprises. Each of my couples gets a Wedding Workshop where we sit together and plan every element of their ceremony. The best service an officiant can offer their couple (besides being unboring!) is a ceremony without unpleasant surprises.

We want to offer an "element-of-no-surprise" guarantee. This is crucial to our couples feeling confident and excited about their ceremony instead of scared and uncertain. The "element-of-no-surprise" means your couple will know every element that's included and everything we'll say in their ceremony.

The very first thing I do when a couple confirms me as their officiant is schedule our Wedding Workshop. Why do I call this step the Wedding Workshop? Isn't there a less onerous term I could use? Something more approachable like "Ceremony Discussion" or "Tea Time with Mark" or something? Sure, I could. I use the term "workshop" deliberately because I want them to come ready… to work. The purpose of the workshop is to get them to think about everything they want in and from their ceremony.

It's important to remember right from the beginning of the workshop that your couple are the bosses. A lot of officiants in my online course community have reached out to me feeling frustrated at the hands-off nature of their couple. Or how their couple want to move something around that they know won't work. Or that their couple doesn't want their story told. The officiant feels upset because they have a vision for the ceremony that the couple are not seeing. And they ask me for advice.

What I tell them is this: you save yourself a lot of misery when you keep in mind that this is the couple's wedding—not yours. It's their ceremony—not yours. If they add an element you don't like, it's best to comply. If they don't want an element that you typically add—

they're the bosses. This will help you relax and remember that this is not all on your shoulders. If you explained why something is best and they veto your advice, it's out of your hands.

That said, when we meet for the workshop, we want our couple to get ready to put their thinking caps on and tell us what they want. That's what I'm going to teach you how to do in this section. You'll be able to walk them through each element, one at a time. There are a dozen ways to do each one, but it's not necessary to dream up every single option. Typically, there are between one and four best ways to do each part. So, we're going to give our couple a brief rundown of what works best and allow them to choose their favourite.

The very first step on this journey is to tell your couple that you're going to meet together. It's best to meet in person, and walk them through every detail of the ceremony. You're going to find out what they know, what they don't know, what they want, and what they don't want. All they have to do in the meeting is decide from the choices you give them.

When I arrive at the Wedding Workshop, I have my laptop with me and I open up a two-column spreadsheet I've designed. The spreadsheet has every ceremony item and element listed out in one column. I type their responses in the second column. To get your very own copy of the spreadsheet as a thank-you for reading this book, visit www.unboringweddingacademy.com/spreadsheet. Then you can follow along hands-on.

I've split this conversation with our couple into five parts so we forget absolutely nothing. We're going to:

1) Start the workshop with a specific strategy
2) Cover the logistical details
3) Plan the pre-ceremony
4) Brainstorm the elements of the ceremony
5) Wrap up the workshop with a specific strategy.

Let's dive in.

ONE: START THE WORKSHOP

Have you ever been called to a meeting or a wedding rehearsal or a gathering with no sense of when it'll end? You feel trapped and frustrated. I'm a big fan of starting meetings and gatherings strong and formally. With a kickoff that lets everyone know I respect and value their time. And most importantly, that I will end the meeting when we planned to end it.

The Wedding Workshop will be a well-run meeting. That's why we don't just jump in. Instead, we bookend the start and the end of the meeting with a very important strategy.

Two Things to Tell Your Couple

These are the two things we tell our couple to start off the workshop. First, we tell them that this workshop is only going to take one hour. Mark the time when you say it. "It's 2:15 now, and we'll be done by 3:15 at the latest." When we set an end time, it makes sure the meeting doesn't drag on too long. It also helps them know that when we get to the more complicated parts of the discussion (typically the processional order), they don't need to worry. This is a routine speed bump, and it still won't go over an hour. We'll blow through some parts of the planning, and we'll get a bit hung up on other parts. It's all part of the hour.

As the officiant, how do you keep it to an hour? Here's how. Let's say we get to an element where the couple doesn't know what they prefer or they even disagree about what to decide. If and when this happens, we're not going to referee them or pull out our popcorn and watch them wrangle it out. Nope. We're going to say, "Alright! Well that's a decision you still have to make. I'll mark that in your script as TBD (To Be Determined), and you can discuss with each other later and let me know." In my experience, even when a couple comes in without a clue about their ceremony and haven't given it any thought, we still come out of the meeting with 85% of the items decided. We'll mark any outstanding items in their script as a TBD. And because we're having this meeting ideally four to six weeks before the wedding, there's plenty of time to make decisions about those last few items on the to-do list.

The second thing we tell them is, "You're going to feel way less stressed at the end of this meeting." Our goal here is to find out what they know and find out what they don't know. It's not to nail down every detail with 100% certainty. Before this workshop, their wedding ceremony is some fuzzy idea of an event that's going to happen on their wedding day. By the end of this meeting, they're going to have a crystal-clear picture of how it's going to go. That's the transformation we're promising them.

We're going to talk over logistics, pre-ceremony vibes, and every element of the ceremony. We're going to be taking them by the hand and leading them into imagining what's happening all throughout their ceremony. Coming out of the meeting, most couples say, "Wow! Now it feels real and I know what it's going to be like!" You can tell them before you start that they're going to feel like it's real and they're going to feel way less stressed at the end. It won't be some big unknown in the future anymore. It's going to be a plan on paper (or screen) that you're going to use to create their script.

We've started the workshop. We've told our couple (1) it's only going to take an hour, and (2) they're going to feel so much better about their ceremony in an hour. Now we're ready to get to work.

Encourage one of them to pull out a notepad or their phone's Notes app to keep a running list of outstanding items. They may want to leave the meeting with a concise checklist of things left to decide coming out of the meeting. We're going to be marking those items in our spreadsheet and on their ceremony script as well so we don't miss a thing.

TWO: COVER THE LOGISTICAL DETAILS

Now we start in on our two-column Wedding Workshop spreadsheet. It lists out all the logistics of the ceremony. Over sixty cells cover everything from the people in the wedding to the mics we use to the songs that will play. After doing this for as long as I have, I've learned that we don't want to take anything for granted or make any assumptions about what our couple want. Our attention to detail comes right down to the proper names of our couple. So that's where we start. And if you haven't yet, get your own copy of the spreadsheet as a free thank-you for reading this book.

www.unboringweddingacademy.com/spreadsheet

Couple's Names?

When you're working with a couple you've never met before, you'd be surprised at how easy it is to only ever see their names in writing (in the initial contact email, back-and-forth setting up the Wedding Workshop, and whatnot). You may never actually hear or say their names out loud until the wedding day. Don't make that mistake. Do it at the workshop.

I was officiating for a French-speaking NHL hockey player and his fiancé Camille. In case you're wondering, I'm aware that's a brag without actually pulling a name-drop. Anyway, back to what's-his-name and Camille. Now, go ahead and say that name out loud. "Camille." How did you say it? Camille with an "l" ending? Me too. In Camille's case, we got to the vows and I asked her to repeat "I, Camille, take you…" I pronounced it "Kameel." She looked at her groom, and said the first word boldly, "I," but then she stopped. Then she looked at me rather sheepishly and said, "Kamee," and shrugged. She kind of giggled apologetically. I'm sure my face turned crimson with embarrassment in front of the star-studded crowd. Only then did it hit me like a ton of bricks. In French, the "l" ending should be silent. (You'd think a guy with the French last name Groleau would have a clue.) I only found out I was saying her name wrong *when we'd gotten to the middle of the ceremony!* I'd already said her name a hundred times by that point in their love story. Oops. She laughed, and in fact everyone laughed, and I made a joke: "Well, if *you* want to pronounce it that way!" She's a wonderfully gracious person, and it was a thankfully lighthearted moment. (Whew!)

But my conundrum was just beginning. Because there was still so much more ceremony to go. Now I was in a bind. Should I pronounce it the way I had been (arguably the "English" way)? Or should I now start saying it the way she says it? I went with the latter, and it was essentially an admission of guilt. This tainted an otherwise amazing ceremony for me. Everyone else probably forgot it. I'm still not over it. I've vowed never to overlook hearing and saying the couple's names before the ceremony.

That's why the first cell of my spreadsheet is "Couple's Names." Ask your couple, "Now, I'm going to be using your names a lot in the wedding ceremony. This is going to seem weird, but I want to make sure I'm pronouncing your names the way you want them to be pronounced. So please tell me your names." You might feel silly if their names are Rob and Meg, but still: you have nothing to lose and everything to gain. What if they want you to call them Robert and Meghan? It will save you from finding out in the middle of the wedding vows that you've been saying someone's name wrong for two-thirds of the ceremony.

Ceremony Date and Time?

Our rule for the Wedding Workshop is to take nothing for granted and make no assumptions. The next item on the spreadsheet is the Wedding Ceremony's Place, Date, and Time. As a professional officiant, I often don't see a couple for a full year after they book me. During the time since we last talked, they may have moved their venue or changed their time by 30 or 60 minutes. So, ask them: "I want to make sure I show up at the right place at the right time on the right day. Where and when is your ceremony?" When they tell you, make note of it. And double-check your calendar that it's entered correctly. Right then and there.

Rehearsal Date and Time?

The next info we want to get down is the rehearsal. One of the factors that decides when we can hold the rehearsal is whether the venue will allow us on site to practise. If the venue and the couple are still hashing that out, then we write TBD on the spreadsheet and they'll get back to us. But sometimes the couple already knows that their venue will not be available for the rehearsal. They're usually quite stressed out about it, too. But we can assure them: don't worry! We can have a terrific wedding rehearsal absolutely anywhere. I've held them in parks and backyards and in 600-square-metre condos, squeezed into couples' living rooms, shared hallways, and elevator landings! All we need to do is practise cueing and walking and standing and nailing down some of the choreographed movements. Anywhere will do if we can create a makeshift "aisle" where we can walk and mark a mockup "front" where we can stand. Usually, the couple will quickly suggest a nearby park or their parents' large backyard or a place like that.

The second factor that's often a concern when it comes to scheduling the rehearsal is who will be in town. The family and members of the wedding party are usually coming in from another part of the country or the world. This is why the most common time to have a wedding rehearsal is the night before. Almost everyone who's in the wedding is in town by then. If a number of friends and family can't be there, sometimes the couple says, "Then it might not be worth having a rehearsal." This isn't true! It's always better to have a walkthrough. If for no other reason than to practise Partner B's arrival at the front in the processional and to go over the vows and ring exchange. That can happen even if it's only the three of you.

If some people have to miss the rehearsal, we just add another item to our pre-ceremony checklist. Having a quick chat with the people who missed it becomes one of our things to do when we arrive early on the wedding day. We find the people who weren't able to make it and fill them in on what they need to do. If possible, we might want to bring them to the front and do a quick walkthrough. There are seldom any guests present thirty minutes before the ceremony. That's the time to show that bridesmaid or groomsman where they need to walk and stand and tell them what they missed at the rehearsal.

Cast of Characters?

We know how to pronounce our couple's names. The ceremony start time is set. The rehearsal date is set or TBD. The next thing we want to do is get all the people listed out at the top of the spreadsheet. It saves us from having to constantly stop during the workshop and ask for names and who's doing what and "who's that again?" Get 'em all down at the top—right off the top. First names only will do! We're getting these names so we know how to address friends and family members during the rehearsal. "Hey you" doesn't make a great first impression. The other reason for getting names is that we want to approach our fellow vendors by name (photographers, planners, etc.) on the wedding day.

Here's what the categories on my spreadsheet look like. We don't leave anyone out.

Photographer(s): (Who's taking the photos?)

Videographer(s): (Is anyone taking video of the ceremony?)

Planner: (Is there a wedding planner the couple has hired for the day?)

DJ/Live Music: (Is the ceremony music provided by a DJ or a

musician?)

A/V Technician: (Who is handling audio amplification equipment and microphones?)

Flower Girls, Ring Bearers, Junior Wedding Party: (Are there any kids in the ceremony? How old are they and what is their designated role?)

Pets in the Ceremony?: (Yep, I've seen a lot of dogs come down the aisle.)

Partner A's Wedding Party: (Bridesmaids and/or groomsmen or bridesmen or groomsmaids… you get the picture.)

Partner B's Wedding Party

Parents of Partner A

Parents of Partner B

A word on the parents above. When we're asking about parents, I find it's most tactful to ask, "Will any parents be attending?" That way we're not making any assumptions that parents are coming. In all my years officiating, I've learned that this can be a most sensitive area. Parents could be deceased or refusing to attend or not be invited. We don't want to phrase the question in a way that assumes they're coming.

Microphones

We've listed out all the people (and animals!) who will be participating in the ceremony at the top of the spreadsheet. Now it's time to get down to the question of how many microphones we will need and for whom. We'll be asking our couple five questions when it comes to mics and nailing down the best option.

1. How Many Guests?

Let's be frank: microphones are a pain, and they're just one more thing that can go wrong in the ceremony. Ideally, we don't want to use them. If we can get away with not using a mic, we bypass all the hassle.

That's why we need to ask: how many guests do you think will be attending your wedding? If that number is 50 or under, I'm not sure you need a mic. Now, there are a couple of variables to consider. For example, if you're broadcasting the wedding via a tablet or laptop and those devices are at the back of the room, then you may need a mic so they pick up your voice. It's hard for people tuning into the wedding virtually (via Skype, Zoom, or some other technology) to hear if you don't have a mic. The other thing you need to consider (and be honest!) is if you have a quiet voice or whether you generally project well. If you're a soft-talker, then you may need a mic regardless of the number of guests.

2. Indoor or Outdoor?

Another major factor that affects what kind of mic we use is whether the ceremony is happening indoors or outdoors. There are three types of mics you might be given: a handheld mic on a stand, a lavalier mic that clips onto your clothing, or a headset mic that you wear over your ear. These are all typically fine—unless the ceremony is outside. Lavalier mics are notoriously terrible in the wind. It's happened often: I'll do a soundcheck before the ceremony, and there's a light breeze. Every few seconds, the speakers just roar. When that happens, we need to ditch the lav mic and find a handheld on a stand or do without a mic altogether. No one wants to strain to hear you deliver this incredible unboring ceremony while you sound like a bad AM radio station. If the couple plan to have the ceremony outside, make sure you tell them that a lav mic is fine, but they need to arrange for a Plan B handheld—and a stand.

3. What Style of Mic for Officiant?

Now that you've walked them through this, you're a bit more ready to make the call on the best mic for the ceremony. Lav mics are the most convenient—they don't get in the way on a stand, and they let you move your head naturally while still picking up your voice. But if it's windy, why not just hold the mic?

Don't do it. Don't even try. Especially if you're newer at this. I've got years of officiating and hundreds of weddings under my belt, and I insist on never holding the mic.

I use a binder that I need to hold with two hands. In Part Three of this book, I'm going to show you how to format the script so it's easy to read. That means you're holding either a big binder or a standard tablet. There's no way we want to be holding our script with just one hand plus a mic with our other. Imagine yourself up there trying to figure out how to juggle and balance your binder or tablet and the mic. And then you need to scroll or flip pages. And maybe you're contending with the wind at the same time and trying to hold down your pages. Nope nope nope—all bad. We want to be 100% focused on the words we're reading and how they're coming out of our mouth. That means the mic needs to be literally that last thing on our mind. I've had some dismal reports from clients in my officiant coaching program on Monday morning. "Mark, I didn't listen. I held the mic, and it was a mess."

The mic stand might be a dealbreaker for some couples who don't want "the ugly mic stand" in their photos. They might insist that you use a lav mic or headset mic. If it's not windy, fine! If it's outside and it's windy, the lav won't work. They'll just have to consider either having the stand in the photos or having their guests not hear you. It's that simple.

4. Does the Couple Need a Mic for Vows?

This is the part of the Wedding Workshop where we want to apologize to our couple for jumping into the deep end of the pool so early in the meeting. But it's time to ask: how do they intend on saying their vows? We're asking because this directly relates to the mic we'll need.

There are three styles of saying wedding vows. Do they want to write and read their own? Do they want to repeat after you line by line? Or do they want you to read them each a big long question and then they take their turns simply saying, "I do"? (More on this in the "Ceremony Elements" section below.)

Chances are, they're going to have a strong feeling about one style or another, and you can just settle it now. If our couple want to write and read their own vows to each other in the ceremony, then it doesn't matter if the officiant has a lav mic or no mic or a headset. They will need to use a mic so their guests hear them read their vows.

If you're using a lav mic in the ceremony, they can't share that with you. They'll need to have a handheld mic nearby that you can give them. If the officiant is using a mic on a stand, then the best thing to do when it's time for them to read their vows is to give them that one. You'll pop the mic off the stand and hand it to Partner A, who can hold the mic as they read their vows. If the couple are simply doing the "repeat-after-me" style of vows or saying "I do," then a mic isn't necessary. Everyone will know what they're saying. That said, sometimes I do hand them my mic for repeat vows if it's a huge wedding.

5. Any Readers who Need Mics?

One more question will decide the mic situation. Is someone else speaking from the front during the ceremony? Is another person coming up to read something or pray or say some words? If not, then we move on. If yes, then again: whether or not you're wearing a lav mic or using a mic on a stand, if there are more than 50 people, that reader will need a mic. There are a few options here to explore further with the couple.

Where does the couple want the reader to stand? Three options. First, they can come right up to the officiant's place, and you will just step aside. If you're using a mic on a stand, they can simply use the centre mic you were using. Another option is for them to walk to the front and use a mic that is set up off to the side of centre by the end of the last groomsman or bridesmaid. Another less common option is for the person to stand and read from their seat. When the couple has decided where they'd like the person to speak from, then we can decide: do we need an extra mic for the reading or is the centre mic enough?

With those questions down, we've decided how many mics we need, what types of mics will be best, and where the mics will need to be at the front. Time to get to the more fun stuff: brainstorming the actual events!

THREE: PLAN THE PRE-CEREMONY

Fifteen Minutes before Ceremony Start

You may think the pre-ceremony is the wedding planner's turf. Nope! It's as much yours, if not more so. First of all, we never want to assume our couple have a planner. Second, if something in the wedding has anything to do with the ceremony, it's our baby. Third, if your couple does have a planner, that planner will love you for showing some competence here.

This part of the workshop is likely the first time your couple has stopped to actually envision those minutes leading up to the ceremony. They usually start feeling jittery right in front of us and making little "whew!" sounds. It starts to feel real. Even the nerves they'll feel on the day start in on them right now. We want to help them think through where they'll be and what they'll be doing. What will the vibe be while the guests are arriving and the vendors are making the final preparations? Here we go.

Will Partner A and Partner B Be Doing a "First Look"?

The first thing we need to establish is where the couple will be when we arrive. We want to determine whether the couple has seen each other before the ceremony or not. If they've seen each other, usually this will have happened a few hours earlier with the photographer. In the hour before the ceremony, they'll be milling around in the same space behind the scenes—or sometimes even mingling together with guests. That's very different from if they haven't had a first look and they're hiding from each other.

Where Are Partner A and Their Party?

Traditionally, only the groom would be out in the ceremony space chatting with guests as they arrive. The bride would be hidden away in a bridal suite until she appears at the back of the aisle in the processional. These days it's more common for the couple to see each other beforehand, in which case they might be in the same room before the ceremony. We want to walk Partner A through where they'd like to be in the 15 minutes leading up to the ceremony. For example, if Partner A is a groom, does he want to be in the ceremony space greeting guests as they arrive? Or would he rather be alone in a room with a best man (and Jack Daniels)? Or with all his groomsmen relaxing and trying to keep his nerves in check? Did he already see Partner B? If so, maybe he'd rather be hanging out with his fiancée and their wedding parties? Give Partner A a sense of those options and what would work best for them.

Where Are Partner B and Their Party?

Likewise, it's most common for a bride to be hiding in a bridal suite before the ceremony, but it's totally up to Partner B to decide where they want to be. Would they like to be away from Partner A, awaiting the big entrance at the top of the aisle? Or would they rather be hanging out with Partner A, basking in the excitement together? Or out greeting guests? Anything goes nowadays, so we help them make the decision that will be best for how they're feeling in the minutes leading up to start time.

Who Is Playing Pre-ceremony Music?

We want to make sure there's a comfortable and exciting atmosphere as guests arrive. One of the crucial aspects of achieving that is to have music playing in the ceremony space. The style of music will set the mood. If it's a solo cellist, there will be a very different vibe than country music played by a DJ. We want to ask our couple who is playing music, and have they thought about what kind of music they want in the minutes leading up to the ceremony?

Who Is Greeting Guests at the Door?

The last pre-ceremony detail we want to ask is whether they'd like to assign anyone at the door. This person will be welcoming guests or handing out programs if there are any. Often, two or three groomsmen will have this job. Other times, the venue will designate a staff member or two to greet guests and direct them to the ceremony space.

Our couple may want to choose who greets guests as they arrive. They can ask a cousin or two, or even the reception emcee, to take on the door duties. Some couples feel it's not necessary to officially choose anyone if there will be enough signs to welcome and direct people. I like to advise them that it's a nice touch to have real live people there making guests feel comfortable, helping them with where to go, and answering the age-old question at weddings: which side do we sit on? (Most couples say that sides don't matter. Pick a side—any side.) If it's a very large site or a hotel where guests have to get to a certain floor, then you almost certainly want to assign someone to point the way.

The final consideration when choosing the greeters: we want two or three people who are friendly but who won't get pulled into long conversations with extended relatives at the door. That means parents and siblings aren't a great pick for this job! They'll start kissing and hugging and catching up, and the entrance to the ceremony will be all jammed up. The ideal greeter is someone who's friendly but not someone who guests will want to congratulate and talk up.

FOUR: BRAINSTORM THE ELEMENTS OF THE CEREMONY

The pre-ceremony details are settled. We know exactly what's going to happen in the half-hour before start time. We know who is where and what music is playing. Now we can brainstorm what happens during the wedding itself.

Ceremony Kickoff

Figuring out how we're all getting to the front can be the most time-consuming part of the whole workshop. Some couples need to start drawing full diagrams on the café napkins to work it all out. It's like cracking the nuclear codes. Others rattle off the plan like they've been thinking about it since they were kids. It's a five-second note. For example, in my early days of officiating, Amber and Cliff and I got together for their Wedding Workshop. We got to the part where I asked them who's coming down the aisle and when. They said, "Oh we're not doing any of that. Just gather everyone to the front of the patio and then ask us to come to the front and join you under the umbrella." Well okay, then—that was easy!

Jessica and Prashant were another story. During their workshop, I asked them, "Alright. Who's walking in and when?"

"Prashant wants to walk up with you, and then the processional will start," Jessica said.

"Nice and easy!" I said. "Okay, so who's walking down the aisle?"

"My seven girlfriends," Jessica said. "Jessy, Eleni, Jessica, Eleanor, Hetal, Dee, and Carol." I typed them all down.

"Okay! Pretty big wedding party! Now, how about you, Prashant? Who's walking in on your side?" He gave me a sly grin.

"Well, there's Aman, Richy, Sukhdeep, Madhav, Navjot, and Ravi, and Ricky." I typed away.

"Alright! So that's your seven."

"Oh, I'm not done," he said, smiling now. "Also, another Ricky. We'll call him Ricky B. And then Mandeep." My keyboard was clicking away. "And Andrew." I looked up at him. My fingers had slowed now. "And Sandeep." Okay, wow. "Oh—and we've got two flower girls coming down the aisle. And Jessica's brother who's not in the wedding party. And our two mothers who we'd like to have in the processional as well." I swallowed hard and started sweating a little.

"So that's seven on Jessica's side and… *eleven* on your side. An uneven number. All walking in?" I asked.

"Yes," Jessica said. "Oh, and we'd like them to walk in together if possible. Like, sometimes two guys with a girl and sometimes two girls with a guy."

I gulped again and smiled. It took us about twenty-five minutes to sort out who was coming in with who and when. In the end, the processional was glorious, but the planning process had been a mess. That happened to me a lot more times in the months that followed. Soon I realized: I need a simplified way to approach the processional conversation. As wedding officiants, we want to be able to guide our couple through who is walking in when and with whom—in the simplest way possible.

There are a ton of ways to organize a wedding processional. We want to stay away from paralyzing our couple with choices or explaining all the possible configurations. At the same time, we do want to inform them of some options they may not know they have. And we also want to prevent them from overwhelming us and each other with a data-dump of names and roles with little or no plan.

I've honed three questions we can ask right up front as a "process of elimination." With these questions, we're cutting to the core of how the couple wants to start the ceremony. At the same time, we're cutting out all the ways they *don't* want to start it. All the while, we're getting closer to realizing their vision.

Is Anyone Escorting Partner B Down the Aisle in the Processional?

Most couples know which of them will be walking down the aisle and whether they want to do it alone or with someone. Typically, Partner A is up there already and Partner B enters in the processional. So right up front, we want to ask, "Are you walking down the aisle, and is anyone escorting you?" For example, if it's a bride, she might say, "Yes, I'm walking down the aisle and I'll be on my dad's arm," or "No, I'd like to walk down alone." When we've determined how Partner B is making their entrance, we've eliminated a ton of alternatives that will muddy the waters and take up our planning time. Now we can ask the next question.

Is Partner A's Party Walking in the Processional, or Only Partner B's?

There are two ways a wedding processional can happen. In the first case, Partner B's party walks in one by one, alone. For example, bridesmaids walk one after the other to the front. In the second case, Partner A's party enters paired up with members of Partner B's party. For example, bridesmaids enter holding the groomsmen's arm, and they walk two by two to the front. Most couples know instinctively whether they'd like their processional to be a single person at a time or pairs, two by two. Once we've settled this question, now we know two very valuable pieces of information about the processional: (1) who is escorting Partner B to the front, and (2) whether Partner A's party will start at the front or enter in the processional.

Is There Special Honorary Seating for the Parents or Grandparents?

Sometimes the couple will want parents to enter as part of the processional. Other times, one or both parents accompany one of their kids—the bride or groom. Other times, the parents will enter as a couple and seat themselves. Sometimes one of the parents will be escorted in because the other parent is accompanying one of the kids (the bride or groom).

There's an alternative to having parents enter as part of the processional: they enter, walk down the aisle, and take their seats before the processional. This is for when our couple don't want Mom or Grandma to be in the processional with the bridesmaids and groomsmen, but they do want to give them some recognition before the ceremony starts. If this is the case, then a typical ceremony start could be (for example): the officiant enters with the groomsmen and stands at the front to signal we're about to begin. No words are spoken yet. Immediately the groom enters with his parents, seats them at the front row, and takes his place. Then the best man enters with the mother of the bride and seats her and takes his place standing at the front. Then the officiant begins the pre-ceremony opening remarks (more on those to come).

When we've asked these questions, we've eliminated a whole lot of distracting options. Now we have a pretty good idea of how our couple envision the start to their ceremony and the processional. We know how Partner B is coming in, we know how the parties are coming in, and we know how the parents are coming in. Now it's time to get very specific.

How Does the Officiant Enter?

We've nailed down those three crucial pieces above. So it's time to back up a bit and establish how we, the officiant, will enter. Are we walking in alone? Side-by-side with Partner A? At the head of a single file with Partner A and all their party? Is there a gap between the officiant and Partner A? For example, sometimes the groom wants to walk in side-by-side with the officiant. The groomsmen will be in a single file behind us. Other times he wants the officiant to walk out front, leaving a large gap. Then he and his best man will walk side-by-side with the rest of the wedding party in single file behind. Get their explicit preference for how you enter and with whom, and you're one step closer to nailing this all down.

How and When Does Partner A Enter?

This may seem redundant after all our hashing out above, but it's such an important detail. We want to make sure it gets its own place on our spreadsheet. After we know how we're entering as the officiant, we want to know exactly how Partner A is entering and with whom. That way there's no room for error and no miscommunication. And the couple are really thinking this through.

Order of Partner A's Entry?

If our couple chooses not to pair up Partner A's party with Partner B's party for the processional walk, then we have Partner A's party enter in single file. They'll unfurl across the front when they get there and stand throughout the ceremony. We need to discuss the exact order in which they're standing from left to right.

This can get quite involved, because there are lots of ways to organize the party. The couple can organize them (1) by height, or (2) by relationship to Partner A, or (3) by their relationship to their counterpart standing in Partner B's party on the other side of the aisle. Guide the couple through these three things to consider.

And then ask them one more question about how their party looks. Do the bridesmaids or groomsmen have anything like alternating gown styles or tie colours that need them to be staggered? This seems like an overly specific or trivial thing. It is not.

At a wedding a few years ago, I had just marshalled everyone at the back: the eight bridesmaids, the eight groomsmen, the parents, the kids, the junior bridesmaids and groomsmen, the ring bearers, and the bride at the back and the groom at the front. It was already

15 minutes past the time we were supposed to start. The guests were sitting in the sun overlooking a meadow. They were turning around, craning their necks in anticipation. We were finally about to begin. It was a star-studded guestlist and wedding party; the groom was a pro athlete. I was a tad more nervous than usual. I gave the wedding party my pep talk like I always do, and then asked them, "Are you ready?" They all shouted back, "Yeah!" Overhearing our cheer made the guests around the corner even more fidgety to get started. And then the bride shouted something you never want to hear.

"Stop!" I looked at the planner. We looked towards the bride. I'm pretty sure we were both white as sheets, and we rushed to the back of the line to ask her what was wrong. "I just noticed when I saw my bridesmaids lined up! They're wearing two different dress styles! We didn't think about that when we were organizing the lineup. The only way they'll look right in the photos is if they're alternating by dress style up there!"

I looked at the bridesmaids. She was right, of course. The planner leaped into action, grabbing ladies by the arm and reshuffling them with the bride's input of who should go where. But you couldn't just reshuffle the bridesmaids. Each groomsman was a bridesmaid's significant other, and they were walking in arm-in-arm. We started grabbing gentlemen and shuffling them, too, according to who their partner was. It was a chaotic five minutes that threw everyone into disarray. And this right when we thought we were seconds from starting. It reminded me of those false starts you see when you watch the 100-metre sprints at the Olympics. I definitely pulled a mental groin muscle with all that upheaval just moments before the ceremony. The result: another vow. From me to myself. *I'll never* not *ask about the wedding party's clothes again.*

With our help, our couple has thoroughly considered the wedding party's heights, relationships to Partner A, relationships to their counterpart standing in Partner B's party, and clothing styles. Now we know the precise order in which Partner A's party lines up at the back, walks in, and stands—from closest to the officiant to the farthest. If Partner A's party is walking arm-in-arm as part of the processional with Partner B's party, you can write this all out further down below when we finalize the full processional order.

Opening Remarks

Before the processional song starts and the ceremony officially gets underway, we want to get in front of the guests, greet them, and set them at ease. That's what the opening remarks are for. The opening remarks accomplish three things in particular. They warm up the guests, they help us feel more comfortable in the space, and they're a time for us to make a couple of very important announcements.

What Is the Couple's Preference about Photo-Taking?

I want to tell guests in the opening remarks whether they can take photos. Couples usually have a gut instinct about cameras and phones out during their ceremony. This is where we get that down so we can tell the guests. If our couple don't want guests taking photos, we'll tell that to the guests: "The couple have asked us to put away our devices so we can be fully present." If the couple don't mind that guests take photos, we'll tell that to the guests, but with a caveat: "Please be discreet and take photos from your seats. The photographers and/or videographers are the pros (and we got their names above so we can mention them by name). We want to let them do their work and not get in their way."

Is There Anything Else the Guests Need to Know besides "Silence Your Devices"?

The second thing we're going to tell the guests in our opening remarks is to please turn off their phones and set all their devices to silent mode. That's a standard announcement at every ceremony, and no couple wants to change that. We tell the couple that we'll wrap up with asking everyone to silence their devices. Do they want us to say anything else? The answer is usually "no." If the couple want you to make some housekeeping announcements about smoking areas or timelines for the rest of the day, we tell them that comes best in the closing remarks. Sometimes they ask that we announce a hashtag for this wedding's social media posts, and we can do that in the opening or closing remarks—or both.

Ceremony Music

After we deliver the opening remarks, it's time to begin the ceremony. My cue for the DJ or live musician is typically, "With that, let's begin," and the processional song is the signal for Partner B's party to make their entrance. At this point in the workshop, we want to take down all the songs that will be played in the ceremony. It's also a great opportunity to advise the couple about the style of song they might want to consider for this kind of ceremony (unboring!).

Processional Song?

The processional song will play for any and all of the flower girls, ring bearers, junior members of the wedding party, Partner B's wedding party, and so on. The couple may or may not have thought about this before the meeting. Technically, we don't need to concern ourselves with what song plays. That's for the musicians or whoever is hitting the play button. It's our responsibility in this meeting to make sure the couple have thought about it and will let their DJ or musician know.

Separate Song for Partner B?

After all the people walking in the processional have made it down the aisle, sometimes Partner B will choose a separate song for their entrance. We want to explicitly ask Partner B: do you intend to have a separate song play just for you? If so, write it down here and make sure they discuss it with their DJ or musician.

Signing Song?

While we're on the topic of music in this part of the workshop, it's best to get all the music down right now. The next song would be the signing song if they're signing the registry during the ceremony (which is more common in Commonwealth countries like Canada). I recommend doing the pronouncement and kiss right before the signing. When they kiss and everybody cheers, then the signing that comes next is really laid-back. We tell the guests we're not done and we'll be right back, and then we go sign at a table off to the side. A fun song plays and the guests and wedding party are buzzing with energy and chit-chat. The atmosphere is amazing! In other weddings (not mine!), the signing happens before the pronouncement, kiss, and the cheer. When the signing is first, everyone is still really uptight and the vibe is pretty dour. Usually, the song is a dirge to match. It doesn't have to be that way. I'll go deeper into this in the signing part of this book.

The most vivid signing memory I have is after I pronounced Kendall and Jim as married. They kissed and we went off to sign with their two witnesses. The DJ fired up the song they chose: "One Love" by Bob Marley. In the three minutes it took us to sign, a party broke out. Guests stayed in their seats but started rocking back and forth and singing out loud and swaying in their chairs—it was incredible! When I came back to close out the ceremony with closing remarks, the vibe was electric and the guests were ready to party! This is the effect that a great song (and inserting a signing if you've never tried it!) can have on what's coming next. For that reason, you might want to tell your couple, "This song can be super fun and get the party started. Choose a song you love!"

Recessional Song?

The last song of the ceremony complements the big finish. We tell the couple that after they kiss (and sign), we're going to make some energy-ramping closing remarks. We'll tell everyone what's coming next, and we'll get everyone on their feet and "present to you for the very first time, _____!" (We're going to say, for example, Mr. and Mrs., or first names only, or husband and husband, as they prefer. More on that when we get to the closing remarks below.) What we're interested in now is coaching our couple to choose a song that comes in really big. This is the musical version of pyrotechnics. The ceremony ends with a bang as everyone sends up a huge cheer and they head up the aisle and take off into married life (or to the bar). Let's get that big song down here. And if it's a song that they love but it doesn't get big til the chorus—no problem! Most DJs can cue it up to the chorus or the part where the song comes in big.

Any Other Music?

Typically, there are only those three or four songs in a wedding ceremony. One song is for the processional, and there may be another separate song for Partner B's entry. There will be another for the signing if we're doing that. The last song will be the recessional song. But we do want to ask our couple if anyone else will be playing a song or singing during the ceremony. Sometimes the couple likes to have a friend or family member perform. If yes, the best place is usually after the vows or after the ring exchange and right before the pronouncement.

Processional

Full Order of All Friends and Family Processing?

We worked through a process of elimination above to save ourselves a lot of trouble at this moment. Now the processional discussion isn't an onerous question to hash out. We've figured out most of the nuts and bolts. We know how we, the officiant, are getting to the front. We've decided how Partner A is getting to the front. We've established how the wedding party is coming in, and we know how the parents or other honorary guests are getting to their seats. We nailed down when and with whom Partner B is entering. Now it's time to make sure we really got it all straight and there were no miscommunications. Review the full order of the processional with your couple, one name at a time. And type it all out.

Kids in the Processional

The last piece to discuss is the kids. We got their names at the start of the workshop. Now there's a crucial decision to make about *when* the younger ones will walk down the aisle. The two options for when the kids come in are:

1) before the wedding party, or
2) after the wedding party and immediately before Partner B.

What factor determines whether they will enter before the wedding party or after? Unlike a lot of the other processional options, this is not just a matter of the couple's preference. It's a matter of the kids' ages—and weighing the likelihood of all heck breaking loose in the aisle.

The first time it happened, I was taken by surprise. I was officiating for Kristen and John, and they'd chosen a cluster of adorable nieces to walk down the aisle as flower girls. Kristen and John wanted the girls to scatter flower petals and herald Kristen's entrance. This meant the girls would come in after the bridesmaids and just before Kristen. Noted and done.

There we were in the ceremony, and the maid of honour had just walked down and taken her place at the front. The three little girls waddled in, clutching their little white baskets. The guests awwwwed loudly. When the cluster got to the last row at the back of the aisle, three-year-old Ava abruptly stopped. Five-year-old Clara tried coaxing her to continue, but Ava shrugged her away. Then she sat on the floor. The guests giggled, and Clara tried tugging her. Ava angrily kicked at her. Clara was unsure what to do next, and started to lose her composure. The other three-year-old, Emily, decided to continue on without them. She was halfway down the aisle when a family member from the front row decided to head up the aisle to comfort the crying Clara and retrieve the oblivious Ava, who was still sitting in the middle of the aisle. The adult picked up Ava, who started crying as well. Seeing the other two of her flower girl cohort being escorted off in tears, Emily panicked. She threw down her basket and started running for her mother, crying loudly and taking a hard left into the seats at the second row. Guests were giggling, three flower girls were bawling, and stray baskets were being whisked off the floor when Kristen rounded the corner on her father's arm. Everyone was struggling to regain their composure and ignore the continuing drama among the little girls and their rattled parents and doting grandparents. Kristen began her once-in-a-lifetime bridal march. She was all too aware of the distractions vying for her guests' and her groom's attention.

I say to every bride and groom that the kids have one job to do in the processional: be cute. There's a 100% chance that they'll nail that—no matter what they do or what their roles are. But early on in my officiating career, I started to notice the pattern. Older kids did fine, but toddlers often had unexpected "moments" in the aisle during the processional. When they did, it took a while for everyone to restore decorum. It was clear that the toddler meltdowns and mishaps—cute as they may be—were negatively affecting Partner B's entrance. No bride wants to enter to wailing kids, upset parents, and guests still chortling from the adorable kid-catastrophe they just witnessed. On the other hand, the perfect buffer to allow for order to be restored is Partner B's wedding party walking down the aisle. The couple of minutes they take walking in set the tone for the perfect entrance.

I decided to start screening the kids' ages in the Wedding Workshop. Then I could advise couples about the best time the kids should enter to safeguard Partner B's entry from the cuteness-chaos that might erupt. Four or under? The kids should probably walk in before the wedding party. Five or older? Right before Partner B is fine. Now you know: the age of the kids determines when they'll walk down the aisle. Your bride or groom will be eternally grateful—even if they don't know just *how* grateful yet.

With that settled, it's time to ask the names and order of Partner B's party walking in. Then we have just one final task: type out the full, definitive list of people walking in and down the aisle during the processional. Start with who comes in the moment the processional song starts. Get it all down—all the way to who's walking in last, all the way down to Partner B and the person accompanying them. Talk it through and type it out so there are no misunderstandings and everything is straight. Then the processional is totally settled. Whew!

How Far to the Front until Partner A Steps Forward to Receive Partner B?

Partner B comes down the aisle, and we need to brainstorm exactly what happens when they do. First of all, where do they stop? The answer here is almost always "at the front row" or "halfway down the aisle." Here's why.

If we stick with the more traditional variation, Partner B arrives at the front row and stops. Partner A then steps forward and hugs or kisses the parent/person escorting Partner B. Then Partner A takes Partner B by the hand, and together they walk the remaining few paces to the front.

In some Jewish weddings, Partner B's parents might enter together and stop halfway down the aisle. Then Partner B will enter alone, join them halfway down the aisle, and the three will walk the rest of the way together.

The "halfway down the aisle style" is becoming a more popular way for mixed families to all participate in the parental walk-down, too. For example, a biological parent might enter, stop halfway down the aisle, and then Partner B enters with a stepparent. At the halfway point, Partner B changes escorts. The stepparent will hand Partner B to the biological parent and take their seat, and then Partner B and the biological parent will walk the rest of the way.

In the case of same-sex weddings, the brides or grooms sometimes want to do it the traditional way: one is at the front and only one walks down the aisle in the processional. But another common option is for both of them to enter in the processional one after the other. Or side-by-side holding hands. Or at the same time down the side aisles and meeting at the front.

When it comes to Partner B walking down the aisle, there are a few options based on tradition. And there are some new twists for modern families and same-sex weddings. To sum up:

1) Partner A is already up there, Partner B walks in alone or with an escort.

2) Partner A is already up there, Partner B's parents enter and stop halfway down the aisle. Partner B joins them and walks the rest of the way.

3) Partner A and Partner B both enter in the processional (a) one after another, or (b) together hand-in-hand, or (c) at the same time down the side aisles, meeting at the front.

When we have a basic awareness of these three most common options, we can talk our couple through what applies best to them.

Is the Handoff to Music or The Question?

Whatever walking option our couple choose above, Partner B is going to get to the front. If it's with a parent, then we need to talk about asking "The Question." When I bring this up to a bride in the Wedding Workshop, she will usually have a strong opinion about The Question —or she knows that her father does.

"The Question," of course, is the officiant's traditional ask, "Who gives this woman to be married today?" This Question hails from a time, centuries ago, where a woman was literally the property of her father, and he would "give" her away for a dowry price. Hence, when we bring this up to our bride, she may say, "Heck no! Nobody's giving me away!" Fair enough.

We can walk our couple through three clear options for The Question. First, we *can* ask the traditional question: "Who gives this woman/man to be married to this woman/man today?" An update on this traditional question addresses the parent by name instead of asking "who?" For example, "Doug, do you give Megan to be married to Rob today?" This modernizes and personalizes The Question a little bit.

A second option is to ask a more contemporary question. Instead of "giving," we're asking about support and blessing. "Who stands in support and blesses Megan and Rob's marriage today?" Like the first question, a more personal version of that question uses the parent's name. "Doug, do you support and bless Megan and Rob's marriage to one another today?" We can ask that to the one or both parents escorting Partner B. We can also ask all four parents or all six—or however many there are if it's a blended family.

The third clear option for Partner B's arrival is to scrap The Question altogether. With this option, the handoff happens only to the processional music; Partner B arrives at the front row with their parent, and they stop. Partner A steps forward. Hugs and kisses are exchanged with the parent. Then the couple walk together to their place in front of the officiant. In the Wedding Workshop, we want to present these three clear options.

We also want to make sure that, if there's a father of a bride involved, the bride knows what her father would like here. I always recommend taking his feelings into account and maybe having a conversation with him about this part of the ceremony. I say this from experience. It's happened to me a few times, but I'll never forget the first time.

In Elise's Wedding Workshop, I asked her if anyone was walking her down the aisle. She said, "Dad." Great. Then I presented her with the three options for The Question. She told me she wanted no question asked. Perfect. The bride gets what the bride wants. I noted it on my spreadsheet.

Then came the rehearsal. Elise and Dad walked down the aisle. They arrived at the front row. Elise's groom stepped forward as per the script, they did the hugs and kisses with Dad, and took each other by the hand. (This part always needs lots of practise.) I directed them to walk towards me and take their place in front of me holding hands. When they were in place, I directed Dad to have a seat. That's when I noticed Dad's face was frozen in pained shock. "Do I not say anything here?" he asked.

"You can just have a seat," I replied somewhat awkwardly.

That's when I knew: Dad expected The Question. He was waiting his whole life for this moment to say "I do"—to give his blessing to his daughter's nuptials. But Elise had told me: no question.

We finished up the first run-through and were getting set for the second and final go. When I looked for Elise and Dad at the back of the line, I noticed they were off to the side having a slightly tense conversation. I looked busy doing something else to delay our start. After a couple of minutes, Elise made her way over to me. "Can we make a slight change?" she asked. "Could you ask the 'support' version of The Question, please?"

"Of course!" The bride gets what the bride wants. And sometimes her family needs to have a little input. That's why we always want to advise our couple to consider the parents' feelings about The Question. Those feelings may affect our couple's decision about whether or not to include it. It can also prevent rehearsal drama. Nobody wants that.

Is There a Bouquet Handoff? To Whom?

As we promised our couple at the outset of the Wedding Workshop, we're leaving no stone unturned here. That means we ask every detail. When Partner B and Partner A arrive at the front, we want them to face each other holding hands. It's the most intimate configuration for when we're telling the story. In order for them to hold hands, they can't be holding anything else. That's why I ask Partner B if they will be holding flowers or anything else as they come down the aisle. A fan? A giant feather arrangement? A hairless cat? If they are, we choose who Partner B will hand that to for the ceremony. They can get it back at the end right before we present them as married and send them up the aisle. The job of holding the flowers (or whatever) can be anyone from Mom in the front row to the maid of honour to the flower girl.

Will Someone Need to Arrange Partner B's Dress?

One last detail before we get to the details of the ceremony elements. If Partner B is wearing a dress, she might need it smoothed out and arranged when she makes that turn to face Partner A. It can get really twisted up when she makes that turn. Typically, the maid of honour has this job. But I've had few brides say to me, "My maid of honour is my best friend, and she's also a hot mess and she's terrible with details like that. I don't want her anywhere near my dress." Um, okay. Good thing we take nothing for granted in the Wedding Workshop! We want to ask who would be best if Partner B needs someone to smooth out a dress as we get underway.

Elements

We've made it to the actual goings-on in the ceremony! The couple are in front of the officiant, holding hands. What now?

Has a Significant Family Member Passed Away Who We Would Like to Acknowledge?

I tell the couple I'm going to kick off by giving a brief lighthearted preamble to the guests before we dive into their love story. But if someone close to the couple has recently passed away, there's something we may want to do before we get to the story. If a close family member or friend has recently passed and their absence will be conspicuous, it's a nice touch to acknowledge our feelings and recognize them by name.

Most couples don't want things to get too sad here. "I want to remember my mom, but I don't want a second funeral," one bride told me. If they say someone has passed away, we ask them if they'd like us to make a brief statement in memoriam. We'll mention how we remember that person, thank them for their role in who the couple have become, and that the person is with us in spirit and memory. We will pause briefly and allow a moment of silence. Then we'll get right into the story and all the laughs and happy tears.

It's best to make the brief tribute right at the beginning. That way the family doesn't start to question why we haven't taken the time to mention that special deceased loved one yet. They won't be distracted wondering if and when we will. Do it right away, and then we can move on into the ceremony elements and getting the couple hitched in a fun and celebratory way.

Every couple is different. Some couples don't want to make too much of the passing of a loved one. Others feel that a brief mention is not enough. If we sense that the couple want to do something more, we can make a suggestion: the couple might want to light a memorial candle as we're reading our words of tribute. This usually results in a longer silence, as well.

Are There Any Readings or Prayers by Friends or Family? Who and When?

We want to ask about readings at this point because in my experience, readings go best after we tell the love story. After we've talked for our ten minutes or so (and I teach exactly how to do this in the next book), we invite up whoever the couple has asked to do a reading.

Heads up about readings. A reading can completely kill the momentum and the emotion that we've built up in the ceremony. After a couple of years of officiating and telling love stories that brought the house down, I started noticing a trend. The worst part of the ceremony was "the reading." The reading has become one of those things that couples think "just belongs" in a wedding ceremony because it's nice and every other wedding has one. But I noticed I had been setting up the reader to fail. Why? Because they had to follow my ten minutes of everyone laughing and crying and cheering the hyper-personal focus on the couple. And then... they had to come up and read a dry poem.

That all changed on the day I decided to be blunt with a bride in our workshop. "Can you recommend a reading that would go nicely in our ceremony?" she asked. "No," I replied. She looked stunned. Then I explained. "Kelly, I'm not going to recommend a passage for a reading. If I do, we're going about it all wrong. The only way a reading will work in an unboring ceremony like this is if the reading comes from your experience! It's gotta be personal—something loaded with meaning for you as an individual or the two of you as a couple. If you can't think of a reading that fits those criteria, then axe it. The ceremony won't need it."

Kelly's stunned look changed to one of excited pondering. "That makes total sense!" she said. She promised to think about it and get back to me.

A few days later, after I shared the script with her and marked "Reading—To Be Determined," she pulled up the shared script (more on this in Part Three) and added to it. She and her fiancée had decided that her dad would do the reading. He would read *Oh, The Places You'll Go!* by Dr. Seuss. On the wedding day, during the ceremony, I told their love story and everyone was raw with emotion from the laughing and crying, as usual. Then I invited Kelly's dad to come up and "share a reading with us." Kelly's dad came to the front and told everyone he'd like to read a short book that he'd read to his little girl hundreds of times all those years ago. A book that made her dream big. And just look at her now. And he couldn't be more proud of the woman she'd become and the man she chose to marry. Then he opened the little board book, and started reading. "Oh the places you'll go…!" There was not a dry eye in the whole place. I've officiated hundreds of weddings. That's one of the only times a tear came close to rolling down my cheek. And from Dr. Seuss of all things! This is the power of a personal reading that comes from the couple, not the officiant.

Don't recommend a reading. And don't just shove one in here because "wedding ceremonies have readings." An unboring ceremony that centres on their love story doesn't need filler. The only way a reading can compete with what you're going to say is if it comes straight from the couple's history and experience. When it does, it's pure emotion. Keep your Kleenex handy.

Any Religious Elements Like Prayers or Blessings by the Officiant or Someone Else?

Every couple has a different level of religion or spirituality in their life. That's why it's best to ask this as a literal continuum: "On a scale of 0 to 10, how much would you like to incorporate religious or spiritual components into your ceremony?" In my case, almost all my couples find and hire me precisely because they don't have a minister in their life. For my couples, this answer tends to be fairly low, somewhere between 0 and 5.

For the "0" couples, it means they don't want anything religious in their ceremony. For the others, though, if they answer "3" or "5," asking them about adding a blessing and/or a prayer hits the sweet spot. A lot of couples will say, "Well, we're not all that religious, but my parents are," or "my grandparents are." In this case, they'd like to add something religious or spiritual to honour those members of their family. For these, I recommend a blessing—for example, "John and Kevin, may God bless you and keep you. May God's face shine on you…" etc. A blessing is not as intense as a prayer, but it adds a sanctifying element to the proceedings. It's perfect for the "less-religious-but-not-zero-religion" couples.

When a couple identifies themselves somewhere around a 5, I ask them if they want a blessing or a prayer over them and their marriage. They usually accept one or the other.

For the couples who say "6 or 7," I recommend both a blessing and a prayer. (I've never had a couple identify as a number higher than that. An "8–10" couple would likely have a pastor or imam or rabbi or some other clergy presiding over the ceremony.)

Where does a prayer or blessing go best in the ceremony? I find the prayer comes best at the end of the love story and our reflection about marriage. Essentially, we wrap up our ten minutes of talking with the prayer for the couple. As for the blessing, the best place to insert that is right before the pronouncement and the couple kiss.

Sometimes the couple will want someone other than the officiant to deliver the prayer or the blessing in the ceremony. That probably came up earlier when we asked them about mics. If it hasn't yet, you can ask if they want you to say the blessing or prayer or whether someone else will.

Are There Any Other Rituals in the Ceremony? By Whom and When?

There are dozens if not hundreds of traditional or ethnic or new or popular rituals we can add to a wedding ceremony. Your couple may want a few or none of these. I always ask, "Is there any ritual you've seen at a wedding that you'd like to incorporate into yours? Unity candle lighting? Handfasting? Sand mixing? Jumping over a broom? Shots? Quaich…?" Some couples look at me like they have no clue what I'm talking about. Others know right away: in their ethnic tradition, they drink scotch from a two-handled cup (Scottish quaich). They exchange coins from hand to hand (Filipino). They stomp on a glass at the very end (Jewish).

Asking about rituals is one of the most intimidating parts of this conversation for new and first-time officiants. If you don't have a ton of experience, you cringe at what they might bring up. You're worried about being "found out" that you haven't done a lot of ceremonies (or even one yet!). You feel like your couple will feel uncomfortable that you've never done a handfasting or broom-jumping before. When I was a new officiant, I used to worry that this was the moment my couple would lose all faith in me. "We'd like a unity potting please." Me: "What the heck is that?" (P.S. It's when the couple plant a tree in a pot together. I've never done one of these, but I've read about it.)

I've presided over at least a dozen different types of wedding rituals. I've had to find out what they were, what to say, and how to execute each one. I can tell you this: it's a cinch. As different couples asked me again and again for a wedding ritual that I'd never done or even heard of, I told them I'd research it. The Wedding Workshop is not a pop quiz! Your couple doesn't expect you to know what a quaich is on the spot right there. If you've never heard of the ritual they want you to do, tell them you'll do the work. Ask them who they'd like to preside over it—you or someone else. You'll go off and research it, write a script for it, and they can have a look and sign off on it. In my experience, that's all they need to hear. Don't be afraid. Honestly ask them if they'd like a ritual.

How can I be so sure your research will succeed? Because it's very easy to find whatever ritual they want on the internet. You're likely to find a full description of the ritual, step-by-step instructions on how to do it, and even full scripting that you can paste into your script. Scripting for wedding rituals tends to be a bit stodgy and traditional sounding. We'll want to take what we find and adapt it into more contemporary language. That way, it fits our style of an unboring wedding. You will find the information you need out there.

In a worst-case scenario, the couple has made a really zany request and you can't find it on the internet. In this case, you can ask your couple to provide a description of the ritual. You can even ask them what they'd like you to say at this part in the ceremony. I've had to do this once or twice for more unfamiliar ethnic rituals. The couple were more than happy to write it up for me. Don't be worried about this, either!

As for where to put the rituals in the ceremony, I find that the very best place for almost all rituals is after the vows and before the ring exchange. There are exceptions for a few certain rituals. One is a handfasting. A handfasting comes best either before the vows or right after the ring exchange; more on that below. Or the breaking of the glass in a Jewish wedding will always come at the end with a "Mazel tov!" But most wedding rituals are a physical symbol of the vows.

Whether it's lighting a candle or mixing sand, they almost always symbolize the inseparable coming together of two into one. Because of this symbolism, it wouldn't make a lot of sense to do them before they say their vows. That's why the best place is most likely after the vows, and then we move into the ring exchange.

The "Big Three" Rituals

While there are more wedding rituals from all over the world than we can count, there are three that recur again and again in Western weddings. I call them the Big Three: unity candle, sand mixing, and handfasting.

Before we get to a breakdown of the Big Three, there's an important piece of advice that applies to all of them. *Make sure your couple knows to bring the necessary accoutrements.* Without the physical stuff, the ritual doesn't happen. You don't want to find out 45 minutes before the ceremony when you arrive that your couple thought *you* were bringing the candles and the matches! You need to spell it out: "As the wedding officiant, *I'm* writing the script and organizing the stage directions. As the couple, *you're* bringing the pieces we'll need."

With that decided, here's a full breakdown of the Big Three. Writing these rituals from scratch can be a pain, so I've also included a sample script you can use for each in the Appendix at the back of this book.

Unity Candle

At the start of the wedding ceremony, there are two taper candles standing with a third pillar candle between them. The unity candle is that single unlit pillar candle that your couple will light with the two taper candles at the same time. This symbolizes two becoming one. Your couple will need to provide:

1) two taper candles,
2) one pillar candle,
3) candleholders, and
4) matches or lighters.

Sometimes the wedding couple are the ones to light the taper candles. Sometimes they're lit by family members. For example, the mothers may light the two taper candles at the start of the ceremony. Then the couple will light the pillar candle with the taper candles during the unity candle ritual in the ceremony. As I'm sure you've figured out by now, all we have to do as officiants is brainstorm a few possibilities with our couple.

In the Appendix, I've provided a sample I use for a unity candle script where the taper candles are lit by the couple. You can copy mine, tweak it, or completely rewrite your own unity candle ritual for your couple. Just know that the flame symbolizes the coming together of two into one. Write something that explains the meaning to the wedding guests, and read it while the ritual is happening.

Sand Mixing

Just like the unity candle, sand mixing is a ritual that symbolizes the coming together of two into one. When it comes to sand, though, there's more of an emphasis on how the two cannot be separated after they've been blended. In a sand mixing, the couple pour different colours of sand from separate vials into one large bowl or vessel. Your couple will need to provide:

1) the separate vials of sand in each colour, and

2) a large, clear bowl or vessel to pour them into.

In the Appendix, I've provided a sample script you can use for a sand mixing ritual. In this particular script, there are four different colours to blend. Two colours represent each of the couple, and two colours represent each family. You can adjust the colours and change the wording to fit what your couple want. Just make sure you write and explain the ritual so everyone observing understands why they're doing this and why it's significant.

Handfasting

"Tying the knot." It's the euphemism for marriage that comes right from the handfasting ritual in a wedding ceremony. The first time I was asked by one of my wedding couples if I would do a handfasting in their ceremony, I agreed, of course. But I was pretty intimidated by it. There are actual logistics to consider! It's not like the unity candle or the sand mixing where the couple do the lighting and the pouring. For a handfasting, the officiant does the work. How do you tie the knot? What do you say?

As it turns out, I had nothing to be worried about. I've done handfasting in quite a number of weddings, and I've modified and adapted a style of handfasting that works well in a contemporary ceremony. It might not work for your grandmother's hardcore traditional tastes or if you need to go by-the-book. But for modern, urban millennials, it turns out beautifully.

Here's how to add and conduct the handfasting ritual to our couple's wedding ceremony. First, choose where to add it to the script. Handfasting works best either just before the vows or just before the pronouncement and their kiss. This is because of the logistics of the couple's hands being tied together. In the "before-the-vows" option, the couple say their vows in their chosen style with their hands fastened. In the "before-the-pronouncement" option, we do the handfasting immediately after the vows and the ring exchange—

before we pronounce the couple as married and they kiss with their hands fastened.

The next thing to do is write an explanation of the symbolism of the ritual in the script. During the ceremony, we need to set up the handfasting ritual by explaining what it is and how it's significant. There's a script for the ritual that you can use at the end of this section.

Third, we want to prepare how to tie a ribbon or cord around the couple's hands. This was the most intimidating part for me when I started out. But it's not difficult at all. A Google search on handfasting will turn up all sorts of ways to do this—dozens of combinations on whether the couple cross hands, hold two hands, just use one hand each, and all the various knots and ties. If your couple have very specific wishes around this, just ask them. They'll take care of narrowing it down. But if they don't have any preference, it's up to you to keep it simple.

Here's what I do. (And there's lots of time to iron out the kinks in the rehearsal.)

1) Ask the couple to hold one of each other's hands—the hands farthest away from the officiant as they face each other. The arms closest to the officiant can relax by their sides.

2) Drape the ribbon or cord over their clasped hands.

3) Pick up your binder and read a few words (see the sample below). Put your binder down.

4) Loop each end of the ribbon or cord over their hands once, then tie a knot underneath their hands.

5) Pick up your binder and read a blessing, prayer, or admonishment, and/or lead the couple in their vows with their hands now fastened. We want to lean into the symbolism we've created here by drawing out the moment a bit.

Finally, we get our couple untied afterwards. This means that when we're tying the knot, we need to make sure the knot is tight but that the ribbon or cord is loose on their hands. If we're doing the handfasting right before the pronouncement and their kiss, then the couple can figure out slipping themselves out at the signing table. But if we're doing the handfasting as part of the vows, then what comes after their vows is the ring exchange. Which means that right in the ceremony, under the watchful gaze of all the guests, the couple will have to get their hands out. We'll want to make sure they can do this as easily as possible and not have to pull a Houdini act. Ideally, they will just slip out of the ribbon or cord without trouble so we can move on to the ring exchange or whatever comes next.

    A good rule to remember is: "yes" to a tight knot, "no" to a tight ribbon/cord. Keep the cord itself on the looser side so they can easily slip it off.

    All your couple will need to provide for the handfasting is the ribbon or cord. In the Appendix, I've provided a sample of the handfasting script that I use. At the bottom, you'll notice two different endings. In Option A, the handfasting happens before the vows. The other iteration, Option B, happens after the vows and ring exchange and before the pronouncement and their kiss. What we say after we tie the knot depends on what's happening next in the ceremony.

Are There Any Custom Elements?

I got a devastating email after one of my ceremonies. Since then, I've added this next question as a separate item on my spreadsheet. The email came from a bride who was upset and heartbroken that I'd left out one of the key moments she and the groom had asked for in our Wedding Workshop.

    "Mark, thanks for the wonderful story and being in such control of all the elements of the ceremony. We were very happy with how it went. But I'm just not able to write a positive review about you. You left out one of the most important things we wanted. Shaun was supposed to address my daughter and commit to fully being her dad after this day. I'm not sure how you forgot to include this, but you did, and we are very disappointed." When I read this, I was gutted.

    How could I have done this? I always send the couple the link to their script (as we'll discuss in Part Three), and I tell them to please look it over to make sure it's 100% what they want. In this case, the bride just trusted me too much, and I'd let her down completely. She didn't check, and I'd forgotten to include it. When I recovered from having disappointed this couple, I went back and checked the spreadsheet from our Wedding Workshop. Sure enough, there it was in the "rituals" spreadsheet cell: "Shaun will address Lily." When I missed that little detail, it meant their ceremony was not everything they wanted it to be.

I was scarred by that experience. Now I have this as a separate row in the spreadsheet. I know I have to check it and check it again. It's a big deal.

If our couple are older and have kids or step-kids and they're creating a blended family, we want to ask, "Do you want to address the kids, make some vows to them, commit to being a parent to them from this day forward or anything like that?" This is often the most beautiful moment of a blended-family wedding ceremony. Make sure they don't miss the opportunity. And don't miss adding it like I did.

Vows Style: Write/Read Own, Repeat, or Simple "I Do"?

In our discussion about microphones early in the workshop, we asked our couple how they'd like to say their vows. If they need some more guidance to make their choice, this is where we help them. There are three styles for exchanging vows in a wedding ceremony.

Style #1: Write and Read Your Own Vows

Some couples just know: they've always wanted to write their own heartfelt vows and say them in the ceremony. Sometimes Partner A wants to do this, but Partner B needs some serious convincing. Here's how we can get them on the same page.

When a couple want to write and read their own vows, the first thing we tell them is that they need to read them in the ceremony, not try to recite them from memory. It's not likely that they are trained actors who like to memorize five acts of Shakespeare and regurgitate them in front of hundreds of people. That's the only way they'd have a chance at memorizing their vows and reciting them successfully. For everyone else, the pressure of the moment is just too much. They need to read. It comes as a relief to most couples when you take away the "memorizing" option.

So, with that established—that they'll be reading the vows they wrote—we have two options from here. These are to prevent them from having to pull out a sweaty wad of crumpled paper from their clothing when it comes time to say their vows.

1) The couple will email us their vows ahead of time (each separately if they don't want to see each other's). We'll format each of their vows to fit on a single sheet of paper. Then we'll print them out, put them in a plastic sleeve, and tuck them into our binder. When it's time for them to read their vows in their ceremony, we hand them their sheet.

2) Some couples opt for wedding vow booklets that they keep close at hand during the ceremony. When it's time, they each read from their book. We'll have the wedding vow booklets ready either in our binder if they're slim, or on a nearby table, or with a member of the wedding party.

The very next question that comes up is "What do we actually say? How do we write the wedding vows?" My answer: don't overthink this. Wedding vows are promises. We know how to make promises. We want to tell our couple: when you sit down to write your vows, fill in the blanks on any or all of the following sentences, and repeat as many times as possible. Make them as funny and as personal or as heavy as you'd like.

"I promise to _____."
"I vow to _____."
"I commit to _____."
"I will always _____."

"Gee, Mark, isn't that overly simplistic? Where's the flowery stuff?" In an unboring wedding, one of the parts we want to include in our officiant speech is what each member of the couple loves about the other. (That's a pro-tip from the next book.) By the time we get to the vows, we've already gushed to each of them on the other's behalf about what they love about the other. If the couple would like to say a few more things they love about each other before launching into their promises, we just tell them not to repeat what they send to us.

The final important piece to consider when it comes to our couple writing their own vows is making sure the vows are approximately the same length. We don't want Partner A's to be a full page and Partner B's to be just two sentences. If they've opted not to see each other's vows beforehand, tell them to discuss and agree on a word count before they start writing. And even when they've told us they agreed on a word count, we double-check that the vows are approximately the same length ahead of time. This is easy if they're emailing us their vows. But if they're writing them in a vow booklet, we need to take a peek before the ceremony starts, or at the wedding rehearsal.

When one partner's vows are much longer than the other's, we want to make sure the partner with the longer set says theirs last. That way, it will sound like the second partner has more to say than the first. No one will think twice about it. The other way, it will sound like the second partner has less to say than the first. This may raise a few eyebrows. Inviting the longer-winded partner to say their vows last makes them look sweet. Inviting the partner with the much shorter vows to go second makes guests think, "Well, that was short!" Let's nip that scandal in the bud.

Style #2: Repeat Line-by-Line

In terms of how much work the couple have to do, repeating the vows is a much "lighter" version than write-and-read-your-own vows. Theoretically, they could still write their own and repeat after you, but typically the officiant provides the vows for this style. Repeat vows can't be too personal. It will sound very inappropriate for the officiant to ask Partner A to repeat, "I promise to give you foot rubs every night," even if the couple wrote it. The guests won't necessarily know that, and it'll be weird. I promise. So yeah, we need to use more generic vows.

"Repeat line-by-line" is the favourite option for most couples I marry. There are a few reasons for this. First, a lot of couples don't like the idea of having their eyes down on a page when they're saying their vows. When the officiant "feeds" them their lines, they get to look right into each other's eyes. Second, couples feel less pressure with this style because they don't have to write the actual vows. They depend on you to bring the words. Finally, repeating vows line-by-line tends to be a more popular option because while the couple don't have to write them or read them, they still get to say the actual words. That's where this style differs from the most conventional style of saying wedding vows: just saying "I do."

Style #3: Just Say "I Do"

For this style, we tell our couple, "I'm gonna read you a 'big long question,' and you wait for me to finish talking. And then you simply say two words: 'I do.'" This is the lightest in terms of work for the couple. All the work is on us.

What's the single most common reason most couples choose this style? In a word: crying. While the thought of getting weepy at a wedding makes us smile, crying is a real issue we need to think about. If Partner A or Partner B (or both!) don't think they can get through talking in the ceremony without crying, we offer to take that worry off their plate with the "I do" style. This is a nice way to say vows because the couple get to look each other in the eye while you ask them the "big long question."

(Bonus!) Style #4: Hybrid

In a more recent ceremony I officiated, the couple read their own vows they'd written and then repeated line-by-line another set of vows I provided. Some couples like to mix it up and combine more than one style. We're not limited to only one style of vows in the ceremony! If a couple are torn between one style or another, offer to do two styles. When it comes to ceremonies, we're only limited by our imagination. When it comes to vows, we're limited to three styles. Ask them to choose one or two and we'll make sure the vows are just perfect.

Who Is Holding the Rings?

If the couple haven't added any rituals in their ceremony, then the next thing to do is move into the ring exchange. This will look just about the same in every ceremony, so there's not much customizing that needs to happen here. The ring exchange looks pretty much the same in every ceremony I write: they exchange the rings and I ask them to repeat a few lines to each other. When it comes time for the rings to be exchanged, the most important question is, "Who has the rings?"

Traditionally, the best man will have both rings because the maid of honour won't have a pocket to keep a ring in. And if there's a ring bearer, it's common for them to march down the aisle and bring the rings to the best man. He pockets them until the ring exchange. But as we've said before, anything goes in the 21st century. It could be a grandparent in the front row, and I even have an officiant colleague who saw a horse enter from stage left with the rings in a saddlebag. Ask the couple who will be holding the rings and we'll add a few "repeat-after-me" words to seal the exchange.

Pronouncement: "Husband/Wife" or "Married"?

At this point in the ceremony, we've gone through all the major elements. I like doing the ring exchange after all the other elements. The only thing that might come after this is a handfasting or a blessing. And at this point in the workshop, we've determined if they want a handfasting or blessing after the ring exchange. We've brainstormed how they want just about every other element of the ceremony. All that's left is to pronounce them married, sign the papers (if it applies), make some closing remarks, and wrap up the ceremony with a big finish.

The traditional pronouncement is made up of three parts: (1) we invoke the governing body that authorizes us to pronounce the couple, (2) we pronounce the couple as married, and (3) we tell them they can kiss. In our case, we're going to say something like, "By the authority given me by the province of New Brunswick, I pronounce you wife and wife! You may kiss your bride!" We want to ask them how they feel about the traditional titles, "husband" and "wife," and whether that's how they'd like us to pronounce them. Alternatively, instead of "I pronounce you husband and wife," we can say, "I pronounce you married!"

Pronouncement: You May Kiss Your Bride/Groom? Or Something Else?

As for the last part of this statement, we want to ask the couple whether they'd like us to say, "[Groom], you may kiss your [bride]," or "[Bride], you may kiss your [groom]!" In the case of a same-sex couple, it's fun to say "you may kiss your bride/groom" because they're both brides or grooms! But of course, some couples don't love the tradition of the officiant telling them to kiss. They'd rather just go at it without our prompting. We want to give them the option that we can also say nothing, which means declaring, "I pronounce you [whatever they decided above]!" And then they just kiss away.

Registry Signing

Now we're at the part of the workshop where we make sure our couple knows what they have to do to legalize their marriage. Do *they* pick up the marriage licence? Do *you*? When do you sign the papers? Who signs them? Are you, the officiant, able to legally register this marriage in this jurisdiction? Do you even need to, or are they getting someone else to do that?

Make sure that your couple–or you–have done the homework and know how to make this legal. You don't want any ugly government-related surprises. Or any miscommunication about who's doing what to make their marriage legal.

If you're the legal officiant, I'm going to recommend that you all sign the papers *during* the ceremony. Now, I've learned that this practice is not all that common in the United States. But before you just skip this part, let me plead a case: it can be fantastic! The signing can add a ton of fun to the ceremony. I love the breather this part of the ceremony gives everyone to chat and start getting loose and ready to party. As we discussed in the "Music" section above, this can be far from a formal whispery affair where everyone is hushed watching the couple sign here… and here… and here, and it drags everything down. It can be the total opposite when we do it right!

Traditionally, the pronouncement comes after the signing. That said, the traditional ceremony was not interested in fun. Here's something I noticed after officiating my first dozen-or-so weddings: when the couple kiss and everyone cheers, all the tension leaves the room. This is no small thing. As fun, modern, unboring wedding officiants, we're trying to get rid of as much of that formality-induced tension as we can. We don't want to eliminate it from the wedding ceremony entirely; a wedding ceremony is formal—and rightly so. The tension in the room comes from the gravity of two people promising to be each other's one-and-only until death. But when does the tension snap like a guitar string? It's when the couple kiss and the guests get to cheer.

When I started as an officiant, I simply followed the tradition: vows, rings, signing, then pronouncement. The couple would exchange rings, and we would go sign the registry. Then we would come back to centre-stage and I would "now pronounce you husband and wife!" or what have you. Everyone would cheer and the atmosphere in the room would completely change to pure joy and readiness to party.

One day I had a thought. What if I could inject that atmosphere of pure joy and readiness-to-party into the ceremony earlier? Like, before the signing?

For my next scheduled wedding, I decided to put the signing after the pronouncement. I never looked back. I've discovered there are a few good reasons to do kiss-then-sign instead of sign-then-kiss, and I always recommend to my couples that we do it this way.

The first reason: the guests can talk during the signing. When we pronounce the couple as married and they kiss and everyone cheers, the tension is completely gone from the ceremony. Here's the practical difference that makes: when I followed the tradition of moving from the ring exchange to signing the registry, all the guests were hushed, silent, watching the signing like it was a solemn exhibition. What else were they to do? Sure, they'd laughed during the telling of the story and cried happy tears and cheered when I'd asked them to until that moment. But the signing was still a "no-talking" time. It had the atmosphere of a library. When I switched things up from sign-then-kiss to kiss-then-sign, I freed the guests to start talking and sharing their exuberance with each other. It was no longer a library crowd. It became an intermission crowd! They were laughing and chatting, comparing what they loved about the ceremony, commenting on what they're looking forward to in the reception. There was a buzz and excitement. In a nutshell, it's way better for the guests.

Secondly, the wedding party can be rowdy during the signing. For the entire ceremony up to now, chances are the wedding parties have been on their best behaviour. Meaning, they've been just standing there. Their role is a symbolic gesture—"standing up" with the couple as a sign of encouragement and support. But when it comes to signing time, it's a lot more fun for the wedding party to be able to chat and interact with each other rather than just stand silently and watch. The kiss-before-signing means they can have some fun too and ham it up in the din of the guests talking and the couple signing.

Third (if you are still not convinced), the music can be more upbeat during the signing when it comes after the kiss. This is something we need to advise our couple about. I used to leave it to chance whether or not the music the couple chose for the signing was a fun song like "Rude" or more dirge-like classical wedding music. But when couples chose violin music for a signing after the pronouncement, I noticed that it clashed with the jovial atmosphere. The music was acting like a wet blanket on a fire that wanted to roar. So now, I let the couple know: because we do it this less traditional way, the vibe is going to be way more upbeat. We want to encourage them to pick a song that's upbeat to match it. And the bonus: all my couples are really happy to choose something fun for this part. Something that's more meaningful to them. Something they've rocked out to together on the radio, rather than the music of an old dead white guy on a harpsichord from 400 years ago.

(Although that can be lovely. Like a few minutes earlier during the processional.)

Fourth, more people laughing means better wedding photos. There are going to be a lot of posed pictures from the wedding day. The photographer probably doesn't need an occasion for yet more of those stiff and wooden shots. They'll get all the photos they need like that from other parts of the day. In my experience with wedding photographers, the occasions for them to capture candid moments of levity are rare. Especially in the ceremony and when all the guests are in their seats. When we do the kiss before the signing, we're providing a windfall of great shots for them. Just about everyone in the room will be chatting and smiling and being more relaxed.

Lastly, wedding officiants can be more conversant with our couple during the signing when there's more of a hubbub in the room. It's way more fun when the couple are talking and laughing and "holy-cow-we're-married!" a little bit during the signing with each other and their handpicked witnesses—and the wedding officiant! When the kiss is yet to come, the couple do the business of signing in virtual silence, acutely aware that the guests are quietly and politely watching them. But when everyone is talking and laughing and the music is upbeat, our couple follow in kind. They're laughing about the ceremony. They're joking with each other about the massive significance of what their signature here means. They're getting hearty congrats from the officiant and their best man or maid of honour or whoever they've chosen to co-sign. This is hard to do when it's dead silent and the couple feels like every word they whisper is through a megaphone and every move is in a fishbowl.

Let's face it: having the signing during the ceremony has a lot going for it. And putting the signing after the pronouncement and kiss has a lot going for it. So, if you've never seen a signing during a wedding ceremony and it's not conventional where you're from, consider putting it in for all the reasons above. And if you're inclined to put the signing before the pronouncement because that's the way you've always seen it, try switching them around for all the reasons above. Okay—now we can get into the nitty gritty details of signing the registry during the wedding ceremony.

Who Are the Signing Witnesses?

The legal paperwork is different everywhere, but in some jurisdictions, the marriage licence requires a witness or two. Check what applies in your case. Then we want to ask our couple who will sign the paperwork along with us.

Will We Be at a Table with Chairs or a High-Top?

Before we get into walking our couple through all the chair logistics and who might be sitting and not sitting, we need to make sure there are any chairs at all! Ask if the signing will happen at a table with chairs or a high-top, cocktail-style table. If it's the latter, then we all just gather around standing. We can skip the next section altogether. If it's a table with a chair or two, then we need to walk them through the sitting bit below.

If Sitting, Do Both Partner A and Partner B Sit? Or Just Partner A?

When I started out, my first questions about wedding ceremonies in general were, "Who sits during the signing of the registry? And when? Does everyone sit down? Only Partner B? What about the witnesses? In what order do they sign?" As it turns out, there are a few ways to do it. Here are five options I recommend (and one that I don't!) for who sits—and when—during the signing of the registry.

Regardless of all the seating options you'll read below, the order of who signs when goes like this:

1) Wedding Partner B (if a bride, "ladies first")
2) Wedding Partner A
3) The maid of honour (or bride's witness)
4) The best man (or groom's witness)
5) The officiant

If it's a same-sex wedding, there's no "hierarchy"; Groom #1 goes first, then Groom #2, and then Groom #1's witness, and then Groom #2's.

Option 1: Two Chairs; Only the Couple Sit.

I'm gonna show my cards here and say I prefer when the couple can both sit. They're on the same level during the signing and they can laugh and chat. Especially when that fun song they've picked is playing and setting the party mood. When we all move to the signing table, the couple sit. They stay seated the whole time, enjoying their first moments as a married couple, and their witnesses sign standing.

Option 2: Two Chairs; First the Couple Sit, Then the Witnesses.

A slightly more traditional way to do the two-chair variation is: both pairs take a turn. The couple sign, then get up and stand beside the table, and then the two witnesses take a seat and sign. When all the signing is done, we move back together to the centre to wrap up the ceremony. This choice gives the witnesses a bit more of a moment in the spotlight. It's an elegant way to honour them if the couple would like.

Option 3: One Chair; Only the Bride Sits.

This style is quite common in the wedding world. If there's only one chair and one person to sit, then it's going to be the bride. The benefit to this style is that the bride takes the focus. The drawback here is that the couple are sort of separated by the height difference when the groom is standing and the bride is sitting. The groom isn't quite sure what to do with himself after he puts his signature on the paper. His bride is sitting and his witnessing friends or family members are busy signing. Honestly, I don't love this option. I usually advise against it. But the couple are the boss and it's their call.

Option 4: One Chair; Only the Wedding Couple Take Turns Sitting

Another alternative is to have each member of the couple sit and sign one-at-a-time. If there's a bride and groom, she goes first, then he goes. If it's two brides or two grooms, it's not a given. (Rock/scissors/paper, anyone?) Then the witnesses sign standing. A benefit here is that each half of the couple get equal attention as they sign. A drawback is that the chair is empty when the witnesses sign.

Option 5: One Chair; Only the Bride and the Maid of Honour Sit.

This one has a traditional and chivalrous flair, as well—the whole "ladies sit" thing. And it's quite lovely, actually—but rarely practised. In this version, we all get to the signing table, the bride sits, and she remains seated when the groom signs. Then the bride stands and yields her seat to her maid of honour (or other bridal witness). The maid of honour stays seated while the groom's witness and the officiant sign.

Not Recommended: Everyone Takes a Turn

I did this at one of my first weddings, and I'm still a bit embarrassed about it. Not that anything terrible happened! It went smoothly. In fact, maybe that's what makes it more embarrassing in my memory. Everyone just went along with what the officiant decided, and it was a bit, well… awkward. The bride slid into the chair, signed, then got up and stood next to the chair. Then the groom slid into the chair, signed, then he got up and stood next to her. Then the maid of honour did the same, and then the best man. Then me. The signing took a long time, and it was a lot of chair-involved movement. Reflecting on this when the ceremony was done, I realized I needed to rethink this. There's no need to do musical chairs as all the guests look on. The most elegant seating process is what we're after, with the most simplicity.

What about the officiant? Do we sit? Because we sign after everyone else, we're not actually part of the melee of signers sitting and standing. We are right by their side the whole time, pointing out where they need to put their X. When it comes to our turn, I'd say do whatever feels best. If the chair is vacant because we've asked only the bride and maid of honour to sit respectively, then it might be natural to slide into the empty seat. On the other hand, if the bride or the maid of honour or both witnesses are still sitting in the signing seats, it's best not to shoo them out of the chair. In that case, I'd sign standing, then invite them to get ready to resume their places at the front.

If you want to skip presenting all those options to your couple, you can. I just tell the couple my preference: that they have two chairs and they both sit. When they're done signing, they stand and move off to the side, and then their witnesses sign. (That was option 2 above.) It's simple and the couple just go along with it. You don't even need to explain it in the workshop. Just put those bullet point steps in the script—as you'll learn in Part Three.

Officiant Gives the Couple's Portion of the Licence to Whom?

I've officiated legal weddings in Ontario and New Brunswick. In both jurisdictions, I had to keep or mail in one portion of the marriage licence, and I had to leave a part of the paperwork with the couple for their records. If this applies to you, I don't think it's a great idea to hand the couple's portion to the groom. He'll just stuff it deep into his suit jacket, party all night, and then return that suit jacket to the rental shop. The couple will never see it again. Yes, that's happened to me when I was a newbie. A few weeks after Bill and Shanna's wedding, I got a call from Shanna. "Mark, did you give that marriage licence slip to Bill?"

"Yes, just like we discussed in our Wedding Workshop!" I said. "I gave it to him right at the signing table during the ceremony. He put it in his jacket pocket. I'll even bet there are loads of photos of him doing it!" Always call in the photo evidence when you can.

Shanna sounded as if she were afraid I'd say that.

"Well, it's not there anymore. And he can't find it anywhere." That's when I decided: I'm never giving that piece of paper to the groom again.

Here we want to ask our couple: "Who is the most responsible person I can give this to?" Make sure they think of a person who will get this back to them safely, in one piece, not covered in red wine stains. The bridal party is usually disqualified due to the lack of pockets in those beautiful wedding gowns. The groom and groomsmen are usually disqualified because of the partying that is about to follow. The most common answer is a parent. We'll most likely give the paper to Mom or Dad in the front row immediately after the recessional or when we find them after the ceremony.

Closing Remarks

After we sign the papers, we come back to the centre, but we're not quite arranged the same way as before. Now we tell our couple that rather than face each other the way they have been during the ceremony, they'll stand facing out. We want them facing their guests, holding hands, and ready to rocket up the aisle when we present them for the very first time. Before that happens, we want to make two very important logistical announcements about (1) what the couple are doing next, and (2) what the guests are doing next.

What Are the Newlyweds Doing Next?

The couple are both the guests of honour and the hosts of the party, which means their presence is kind of a big deal. This also means their absence is an even bigger deal. After the ceremony, our couple may need to head out for photos with the photographer or duck into a private room for a breather. We want to tell the guests not to look for them for a little while. If our couple would like to stay for a receiving line then the guests need to know that, too. Or sometimes in a less formal wedding the couple plans to be the first ones to the bar and they want all the guests to join them there. Whatever they're doing next, we want to fill everyone in on whether they're staying or going so guests know where to find them or to know not to look for them.

What Do the Guests Need to Do Now?

The second thing the guests need to know is what they're doing next. Are they heading into a cocktail hour? Do they need to form up for a receiving line? Are they supposed to drive to another location for the reception? What time is that? Here, we ask our couple exactly what's happening next for the guests and we'll tell them.

We're not going to make this an excruciatingly detailed instruction that deflates the simmering energy in the room at the end of the ceremony. We're going to keep it super high-energy. It's going to be brief and concise. We're saying just enough so every guest knows exactly where to go next and what to expect when they get there, and what's going to come after that. We also want to ask our couple whether they'd like us to tell the wedding guests the exact time the reception starts or whether to keep it open. Couples usually have a strong preference, either "We definitely want a hard start at 6:00," or "Let's keep it open so we're not stressed out about hitting a certain time."

Now we're clear on the logistics of what the couple are doing next and what the guests are doing next. With that, we're ready to wrap this up and present our couple for the very first time as married.

Wording for the Presentation of the Couple?

This is the big moment. The vows were the crest of the ceremony, and this is where that wave breaks and the guests leave totally amped and ready to celebrate. We get everybody on their feet and say, "Friends and family, please stand with me now, it's my honour to present to you for the very first time..." Who? We want to ask explicitly in the Wedding Workshop: how do you want me to present you to the world for the very first time?

There are typically two options. In the first option, we can use titles and their desired last name. For example, if Sally and Sarah are just married, we might say, "Mrs. and Mrs. McIntosh!" Or they might have decided on a hyphenated new last name, so maybe it will be "Mrs. and Mrs. McIntosh-Smyth!"

The second option might be to use no last names—only first names. In this case we will say, "Sally and Sarah as wife and wife!" We want to ask our couple if they are comfortable with the titles "husband" or "wife." It's likely going to be one of those two options that resonates with our couple. And this is how they're making a statement to everyone—or not making a statement—about how they'd like to be addressed as a married couple.

Just a quick word if it's a female/male couple getting married here. Typically, whenever we say the couple's name in the ceremony, we say her name first, then his: "Naomi and Mark." This is true every time we state their names in the ceremony—except for when we use first names for the presentation. The reason for this is mostly grammatical. What I mean is, we more commonly say "husband and wife" rather than "wife and husband." The latter way just sounds a bit inconsistent. To keep the roles respective of who's who, we need to say "Mark and Naomi as husband and wife!" so that Mark is the husband and Naomi is the wife. If we say "Naomi and Mark as husband and wife," then it sounds like Naomi is the husband and Mark is the wife. This is a minor point, but it's also the very last line of the ceremony. We really want to stick the landing and not end with something that makes guests think, "Huh?"

Recessional

We've made the presentation in our best "Let's get ready to rumble!" voice, and the ceremony is over. The big song comes on, and our couple heads up the aisle together. That's a given, but we want to ask the couple: if there's a wedding party, do they head up the aisle two by two—maid of honour with best man, then the next pair, then the next pair, etc.? Usually, the answer is yes.

The very last question we want to ask is, "Where are the wedding parties heading? Do you want them to follow you close on your heels for photos? Or do you want them to head to the cocktail hour and leave you two alone for a few minutes?" When we know this, we tell the wedding party in the rehearsal exactly what their destination is when they head up the aisle after our couple. And with that, we're finally out of questions!

FIVE: TELL YOUR COUPLE WHAT'S COMING NEXT

With any luck and a bit of skill, we've stuck to moving through the workshop questions and providing our couple with a brief explanation of their options at each element. We should be able to look at our watch now and confirm: "And just like I said, that was one hour!" They'll be so impressed that we covered so much ground in just an hour. What's more, they'll love that in just an hour, we took their ceremony out of fuzzy imagination-land and into reality. We got everything they wanted down in black and white. Now they can actually envision how it's going to go.

This quick and early win is no small thing. Your couple is rooting for you. They want you to do a fabulous job and to provide an expert hand at guiding them through planning and executing their ceremony. When you can deliver on this—something as simple as finishing this meeting on time—their confidence in you grows.

That's why the next thing we say is, "How do you feel now?" It's a safe question, because there's no way they don't feel way better than an hour ago. As I said before, I believe in the power of "bookending"—pointing to the way something was and bringing attention to how it's transformed for the better since then. When they sat down an hour ago, they felt a bit stressed. Now, they're excited because you walked them through the ceremony and it feels so real. And a lot of their stress has disappeared.

When they tell you they feel better about the ceremony now, you tell them that we just need to clarify all the TBD items before we go. Remember how we suggested they pull out a notebook or a Notes app at the beginning of the workshop? Now we cross-reference the TBDs and question marks in our spreadsheet with their notes. We want to be sure—and we want them to be sure—about what decisions need to be made coming out of this meeting over the next few days or weeks. Of course, when we send them their script, all the outstanding times will be clearly marked. (More on that in Part Three.) But if they want to leave the meeting with a "to-do" list and a sense of what they need to discuss and settle, this is when they can get those bullet points down. I like to turn my laptop around here and show them my spreadsheet. We look for question marks, we run down the outstanding items, and leave the meeting knowing exactly what's left to decide.

The last thing we tell our couple before we pack up is that they're going to get an email from us over the next few days with their full wedding ceremony script. This will be the script we're going to build from the notes we took in this meeting. It's likely that 90% of the logistics and details and elements are nailed down now. But any of those outstanding items will be clearly marked in the script. They can get back to you with their decisions about those items over the next couple of weeks. They have from now to the rehearsal to nail down what's left. Then it's handshakes and hugs and "see you at the rehearsal." The rest of our work is all behind the scenes until then.

PART THREE: WRITE THE SCRIPT

When you get home from the Wedding Workshop, you hold the hopes and dreams for your couple's perfect ceremony in the palm of your hand. Right now, of course, those hopes and dreams are all in spreadsheet form or scribbled out on a legal pad. Now we're going to take all those rough notes and transform them into what they really want to see: their wedding ceremony script.

START THE ONLY SCRIPT YOU'LL EVER WRITE

I learned this the hard way in my early years of public speaking. When I started out, I'd write a rough outline in Microsoft Word's default format. Then I'd write a rough draft. Then I'd write a new rough outline for my lectern notes with new formatting. Then I'd practise, figure out where the rough patches were, and write another polished outline. By the time I got up to the podium, I'd practised from several different-looking outlines and drafts. While I was presenting, I couldn't picture my notes or where I was in my talk. That meant I had to look at my notes way more often.

I fixed that. Now I make only one outline from the very beginning. Yes, it will go through revisions. But it won't be all new every time. I don't change the format.

I noticed a difference right away. I could almost "see" my notes even when I wasn't looking. By practising with just one set of notes from the beginning, I had subconsciously memorized how the page looked. I could remember where I was without constantly checking.

I've taken that same idea into writing a wedding script. I encourage you to do the same. Don't write a junk draft and then a rough draft and then your final draft for your binder. Save yourself a lot of work and build your official script right away—the actual script you'll read in the ceremony.

MAKE THE SCRIPT LOOK LIKE A PLAY

When you get a BA in English Lit like I did, it means spending four years writing about books and plays. In my second year, I went to the university bookstore and slapped down about a hundred American-Eagle-earned dollars to buy the ten-inch-thick collected works of William Shakespeare. The book the prof assigned was unabridged and expanded in every way. Not only did it contain all the dialogue that the characters actually speak, it was also chock-full of stage directions. Who enters where, who's on the stage, who leaves on what side of the stage, and so on. When the assigned reading for the week is a hundred pages of Shakespeare, you just want to get it done. And all these annoying notes and extra words are in the way. It annoyed me then. I wasn't reading these plays like an actor or a director. I was reading like an undergrad student who wanted to hit the last page of his reading for the week. But if someone had put me in charge of directing the actors and coordinating the rehearsal for *The Tempest*, you can bet I would have been super glad for all those stage notes!

As the officiant and writer of this ceremony, you are the director of the play. That means writing the stage directions will be as important as writing the words you and the couple will say. And it's not possible to overdo it. It can even save the day.

A couple of weeks ago, I emailed David, one of the members of my online course, on Monday morning. David had written his first Unboring!Wedding script from my training, and I'd read his script and we'd had a coaching call. I knew he was 100% ready, and his script was terrific. I was so excited for him to deliver the best ceremony ever, and I wanted to follow up and ask him how it went over the weekend. His answer floored me.

He told me that right after we'd had our call, he got a torn retina in his eye, which caused him to lose his vision. Long story short: after eye-saving laser surgery and complications, his doctor prohibited him from traveling anywhere. David had to make the agonizing and disappointing call to his couple and tell them he was out of commission. They were devastated. But David had a plan. David told his couple that while this was terrible, it wasn't a total loss. The script was fully written. And the way he'd written it, everything was in it. From the songs to who comes in where to their love story and every word he was going to say.

David suggested that he call their mutual friend who was going to attend the wedding as a guest. He could ask the friend to simply step in for him and follow the finished script. The couple agreed that the friend would be great for the role, and David made the call. The friend agreed. David sent him the script with a day to spare. The friend practised it, led the rehearsal from David's detailed script, and delivered the ceremony like an absolute pro. That's what happens when you have a detailed script—the kind that lists everything.

We want to tell our couple what their script is going to look like. In my case, I tell them it's going to be detailed, with bullet points in blue font for every entrance, movement, and standing position. The speaking parts will be in black font, indicating who is saying what and when. And then I tell them, "I could get hit by a bus on Friday, and someone else could deliver the ceremony of your dreams on Saturday, just like I would." (Thankfully, it hasn't happened yet. But I've said this so many times that I always jump when I see a bus on Fridays.)

Write your script like you were directing a play. When you start moving through your notes from the Wedding Workshop, list everything that happens. If the wedding starts at 4:00PM, write that at the top. Then type a heading that says, "3:30." List everything that's happening from 3:30 to 3:55. Who's greeting guests? Who's playing music? Where's Partner A and their party and what are they doing? Where's Partner B and their party and what are they doing?

After you've written all that out, make a new heading for 3:55. List everything that happens then: who's lining up at the back in what order. Then 4:00. Who walks in first and with whom? What happens after that? What are your opening remarks? Remember, this is all in your notes from the workshop. You're making it super organized and easy to read for your couple and for your own script on the wedding day. Use bold headings for each element of the ceremony, and write all the movement, entrances, seating, and standing that happens at each element. (Shameless plug here: my premium online course Unboring!Wedding Academy includes my own pro script and templates so you can simply copy, print, and adapt.)

Detail is king. May you never get hit by a bus, and may your eyeballs forever remain intact. At the same time, a highly-detailed script is like buying life insurance. You hope someone never needs to make a claim, but everyone sure is glad you had insurance if they do.

MAKE THE SCRIPT EASY TO READ

Public speaking always tops the lists of people's worst fears. As wedding officiants and celebrants, though, we have an advantage. In most public speeches and presentations, it's considered a no-no to read every word of your talk. But for us, it's the opposite: it's actually more expected than not that an officiant will read the ceremony.

I have good news for you: you absolutely can and should read the wedding ceremony script word-for-word. We're wedding officiants, not motivational speakers. We're not Tony Robbins. We don't need to stalk up and down the stage and pace back and forth. Nobody expects that or wants that from an officiant. We need to think about officiating a wedding more like giving a presidential speech. Absolutely everything is prewritten. Every word. And the speaker stands in once place and reads it—really naturally, and really well.

There are ways to read well, and there are ways to read badly. A truly great orator reads the teleprompter or the script in the lectern with a well-paced cadence and tempo. This allows her to look up comfortably, move her head side-to-side, and perhaps most importantly, stand tall. Reading badly is the opposite of that. Robotic voice. Eyes down. Scrunched-over posture. Disconnected from the audience.

As wedding officiants, we need to go all "truly great orator" style:

stand and read with a well-paced cadence and tempo. Look up frequently and comfortably at our couple and their guests. Move our heads freely. And stand tall.

If we're going to feel comfortable reading, the first thing we need to do is to type our wedding script in a large font. The default font size in word-processing software like Word or Pages or Google Docs is usually 12 points or even smaller. We love default settings. We rarely question them. And we usually don't even think to change them! I mean, it's the default for a reason, right? A 12-point font is perfect when you're printing a report, but it's a big problem when we're printing out a speech.

The key to reading naturally is not having to stick the page six inches from our eye. It's being able to glance down without moving our head down or moving the script up. It's seeing the words clearly. Thankfully, the fix here is easy: use a bigger font than Word or Pages or Google Docs suggests. The number will vary depending on how well we do at the optometrist. It will also depend on the font we use.

Choosing the right font and size for you will do two things. First, it will maximize how well we can see the words of our script. Second, it will minimize how often we have to turn the pages. We don't want to be flipping paper like we're cramming for a test up there. We want to strike the perfect balance between seeing the words easily and not having to flip pages too often. For me, that perfect balance is Arial 14. The perfect balance for you may take some experimentation. It might be Arial 14. It might be Helvetica 16. Just try to figure it out in your practise runs, not up there in front of the 200 people for the first time. Now that we've resolved the issue of needing a magnifying glass to read our script, we're still not out of the woods.

The next thing we want to do is break up the wedding script into lines. It doesn't matter if the font is big. If we keep losing our place on the page, then we lose all the gains from an easy-to-see script. A script that's easy to see is still not necessarily easy to read. Let's make our script easy to read, too. We do that with a little formatting trick.

A lot of wedding officiants write their scripts in big block paragraphs of text. Why? Because that's how most of us learned to write prose in school. ("Default mode" strikes again!) We feel weird writing in broken lines because—isn't that just reserved for poetry?

Writing a wedding script that's broken up into lines serves a crucial function. It allows us to feel comfortable looking up, looking around, smiling and laughing. We can engage the reactions of our couple and their guests, and seamlessly get back to reading. And then we're not worried about losing our place!

I advise writing the script in broken lines instead of paragraphs. When we do that, we know the last word that came out of our mouth, and we know where that last word is on the line and on the page. Format the script with ten to twelve words per line. That way, when Grandma laughs so hard you just have to look, you can. After you do, you'll easily find the last word you read. There are some reactions in the ceremony we just won't want to miss.

Here's what my script looks like on the page:

Friends and family, here we are!
Scott and Kelly are here today to get married
and they are just perfect for each other.
(Can I get an 'amen' to that?)

But how did we end up here today?
How did these two wonderful people
somehow not only meet,
but also fall in love,
and then choose to spend
the rest of their lives together?

Well, I'd like to spend the next few minutes
telling you one of the true versions
of how Kelly and Scott got here today.

See how easy that is to read? When key words fall at the start and end of the lines, you'll never get lost in a sea of words. Your script becomes a line-by-line map you just need to follow.

CLEARLY MARK THE OUTSTANDING ITEMS

As we build the script and move through our notes from the Wedding Workshop, we're going to come to those places where our couple just didn't know. Didn't know a song, didn't know if Dad wanted to answer The Question, didn't know what mics would be on site. Our Wedding Workshop left no stone unturned, and our script won't either. We want to highlight those undecided items and comment on what needs attention.

For example, a bullet point in the script will indicate "Processional Song Starts." If they didn't know what song would start there, the highlight and comment in the margins will be "Song To Be Decided." Later in the script, another bullet point says, "Couple, officiant, and witnesses move to the signing table." If they hadn't decided on their witnesses in the Wedding Workshop, we highlight the word "witnesses" and comment in the margins, "Witnesses To Be Decided." When we do this for each undecided detail, our couple knows exactly what they need to nail down. Clarity is king and nothing falls through the cracks.

USE COLLABORATIVE SOFTWARE AND SEND THE SCRIPT

We make TBD comments in the margin because we won't be the only ones seeing this script. We're not talking to ourselves, here. Our couple will be seeing this very document, as well! There are ways to share a document so someone else can see and edit the very same document right along with you. This is what we want to use with our couple. I want to make the case here that you write your script using collaborative software.

I recommend Google Docs. There are three immediate and tangible benefits to Google Docs. It's the perfect choice for wedding officiants. First, in Google Docs we can build and share the wedding ceremony script with our couple. Before collaborative, free software like Google Docs became widely available, wedding officiants had to write the ceremony script in a Word doc, then email it to the couple. Then the couple would mark it up and send it back, and then the officiant would make changes and send it back, and then the officiant would have to make a final version that's easier to read, and so on. That's not even mentioning all the trouble that could happen if the Mac people ran into formatting trouble when the file got to the Microsoft people! There's a lot that can be frustrating about the back and forth.

With Google Docs, there's no sending files. We and our couple simply access the same document. First, we write the first draft of our wedding ceremony script in Google Docs. It's the very same script we're going to use when we deliver at the front. It's the only script we'll ever make. Then we clearly mark the TBDs by highlighting the relevant lines and writing short comments in the margins. Next, we go to the document's "Share" options and make it accessible to "anyone with the link." Then we copy our script's unique link, send that link to our couple, and voila! They have their script! We can react and reply to our couple's comments and edits as they make them, maybe even in real time!

It's that easy, and it's great for both our couple and for us. Who wants more emails and text messages? Not me! And neither does your couple. They've got enough going on with the florist and the caterer and the planner. They'll love you for staying out of their hair! When our wedding ceremony script is in a Google Doc, we have a working "hub" where the collaboration is nice and clean. No extra emails and texts on our other messaging platforms. We each check in on the Google Doc periodically and watch the edits roll in.

The second thing that makes Google Docs great: our couple can share their wedding ceremony script with their planner and/or photographer and/or DJ. All they do is send them the link. Their vendor can look at the script you're all working on. It's so helpful for vendors to be able to see exactly what's going to happen in the ceremony. When they know what we are going to do and say, they know how to work around us and with us. It helps them map out the important pacing and logistical elements so they can do their jobs before, during, and after the ceremony. When we share the wedding ceremony script with the vendors, we're in their good books before they even meet us!

The third thing that makes Google Docs so perfect is that we can easily share the wedding ceremony script with a fill-in officiant (remember David and the tale of the torn retina?). In my meeting with any couple before they sign on with me as a client, they usually ask me a pointed question. "What happens if you get sick and can't officiate on the wedding day?" When we have every single word and element of the wedding ceremony script in a Google Doc, here's how we can answer that question:

"If for whatever reason I'm bed-bound on your wedding day, we'll call someone who we know will ace this. All they'll have to do is open our wedding ceremony script in Google Docs. They can rehearse the ceremony we've created together, and then read it in the wedding ceremony. Simple. You'll barely notice I'm not there." Okay, that last line isn't entirely true (cue the single tear if it is), but when the couple hear this, they feel like they're covered from one more wedding disaster—even if a bus jumps out at me on a Friday. (Okay, I'm calling a therapist now.)

The collaborative, real-time, shareability of a program like Google Docs makes it ideal for wedding officiants. It sure beats sending that wedding script back and forth in email attachments. And it gives you and your couple total peace of mind.

Send off that link to your couple. They've got your ceremony script, and you've got theirs. You're all quite literally on the same page. Now *that* feels good.

NEXT

When you sat down to read this book, you had a vague sense of what a wedding ceremony looked like. The Classic 10-Part Ceremony in Part One made it crystal clear. With that foundation laid, Part Two taught you exactly how to walk into any Wedding Workshop with any couple getting married. Now *you're* the guide, talking them through all the most common options of a classic ceremony with confidence. But not just that! You know about all the tricky things to consider, too: mics, readings, to sign or not to sign (that is the question!), and so on. Plus, you're ready to ask them all about custom options: what elements and rituals do they want to add? And you know just where those rituals go best. In Part Three, you learned how to write, format, and share the script they've always wanted.

You've gone from Wedding Zero to Ceremony Hero! You hit the mines and you've come home with the gold. But did you know there's a lot more gold to be had? So *much* more that it would be wrong for me not to tell you about it.

Your next step is to take this customized script and rock it to the next level. To go from "that was a lovely ceremony" to everyone raving about how you engaged the guests just the right amount, told your couple's love story and "love abouts," and made 'em all laugh and cry like the master of the craft. That's my Unboring!Wedding Formula

—the next part of this system. And I'm going to break it down and teach you how to do it—step by step. This ol' wise man, grizzled veteran of hundreds of ceremonies, has a few more cards to show you. Give your camel a short rest, and I'll see you in the next book. You're about to go full Picasso.

APPENDIX

SCRIPTS FOR THE "BIG THREE" RITUALS

A Sample Unity Candle Script

Officiant: Partner A and Partner B, you've just made a lifelong commitment to share the rest of your lives with each other. Today you come here from two families and two stories. And so, as a symbol of these two families and stories becoming one, I invite you both to come forward and light the individual candles. These two candles represent your two families and two stories.

Partner A and Partner B come forward to the table and light the taper candles with matches.

As officiant is reading the script below, Partner A and Partner B each take a taper candle and light the centre candle together.

Officiant: We are especially grateful for the loved ones who have nurtured and invested in Partner A and Partner B and pointed them along in their individual journeys. The family legacy that Partner A and Partner B bring to this relationship will continue to be an important part of their lives and their marriage. And now, they share their family and their stories with each other and with everyone in their circle. From their two families, a new family is created. This is the symbolism of the unity candle. Just as the two individual candles merge into one, the two families in this marriage merge into one here today. From this day forward, Partner A and Partner B shine together with the light that they've been given by two families who love them, now become one.

A Sample Sand Mixing Script

Officiant: Partner A and Partner B, you've just made a lifelong commitment to share the rest of your lives with each other. Your growing relationship can be put into symbol by pouring together four colours of sand. The emerald sand represents you, Partner A, and all that you were, all that you are, and all that you will ever be. The dark blue sand represents you, Partner B, and all that you were, and all that you are, and all that you will ever be.

Partner A and Partner B move to the table.

Officiant: But we acknowledge that in marriage, we are not just coming together as individuals. We are coming together and uniting in community, particularly, in two families' stories blending together, as well. And so the light green sand represents Partner A's family, and the light blue sand represents Partner B's family. As you each hold your sand, the separate colours represent your lives up to this moment, and your families: individual and unique.

Partner A and Partner B pour the sand.

Emerald Green sand (represents Partner A)—poured by Partner A.

Dark Blue sand (represents Partner B)—poured by Partner B.

Light Green sand (represents Partner A's family)—poured by Partner A.

Light Blue sand (represents Partner B's family)—poured by Partner B.

Officiant: As you combine your sand together, we have this wonderful symbol of how your lives join together today as one. Just as these colours can never be separated and poured again into individual containers, the same is true of your marriage and your families. None of you will ever lose your uniqueness—your own particular colour, so to speak. You never lose who you are. At the same time, the merging of your lives and stories will never again be separable, and today you're creating something new and beautiful.

A Sample Handfasting Script

Officiant: A wedding ceremony is mostly about symbols. Symbols are important and helpful, because symbols take an idea and a value we hold and make them concrete and physical. Symbols make concepts something we can see and touch. They're helpful because they serve as a powerful reminder of a time and a place and a memory—a feeling and even a promise—that may have faded over time.

Officiant drapes the ribbon over their hands with the ends hanging down.

Officiant: Handfasting is a symbol like this. It's one of the world's oldest wedding traditions and it's found in cultures all over the world. In joining hands, Partner A and Partner B symbolize how they freely offer their lives to one another. And in fastening their hands together, the cord symbolizes how Partner A and Partner B leave this place today with their lives bound up together. Today, two stories come together and two sets of hopes and desires for the future become joined in commitment and intention.

Partner A and Partner B, as I fasten your hands together and tie the knot, I invite you to reflect on the joy and responsibility that awaits you. From this moment forward, you are bound together in the commitment and intention of marriage. This knot is a symbol of how the bond you make today will never be easily undone.

Officiant loops the ribbon over twice and ties the knot underneath the hands.

Ending Option A: Handfasting Before the Vows

Officiant: Partner A and Partner B will now make promises to each other we traditionally call "vows…"

Ending Option B: Handfasting After Vows and Ring Exchange and Before the Pronouncement and Kiss.

Officiant: Now, with great joy, in front of all your closest friends and family, by the authority given to me by the province, I pronounce you married!

ACKNOWLEDGMENTS

Thanks to my writing coach, editor, and brother-from-another-mother, Stephen Burns; your encouragement, advice, and editing skills made this book happen. Sarah Henderson, thank you; your eye for detail and patience as you edited this book was beyond what I thought possible. Bennett Paris, thank you; it was you who believed I should write a book, and your generosity in editing these pages and sharing your feedback was a true gift.

ABOUT THE AUTHOR

Mark Allan Groleau is a full-time, professional wedding officiant and the founder of Unboring!Wedding. He creates and delivers unboring wedding ceremonies by the sea in New Brunswick, Canada. Mark has helped thousands of emerging officiants and celebrants all over the world get rave reviews through his course, coaching, videos, and articles. When he's not doing wedding stuff, he can be found hiking and beach-combing Atlantic Canada with his family. And sneaking off for the odd round of golf.

facebook.com/unboringwedding
instagram.com/unboringwedding

ONLINE COURSE

Special Offer: dive deeper and join Mark's premium online course for new and leading-edge wedding officiants and celebrants.
www.unboringweddingacademy.com